THE WICKED MR HALL

ROY ARCHIBALD HALL

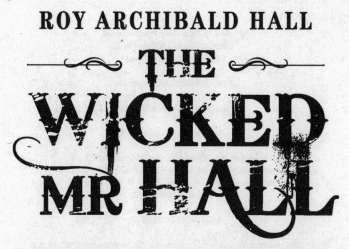

THE WICKED MR HALL

THE DEATH-BED CONFESSIONS OF SERIAL KILLER ROY ARCHIBALD

JOHN BLAKE

605 7660.

Published by John Blake Publishing Ltd,
3 Bramber Court, 2 Bramber Road,
London W14 9PB, England

www.johnblakepublishing.co.uk

www.facebook.com/johnblakebooks ☐

twitter.com/jblakebooks ☐

First published in hardback as *A Perfect Gentleman* in 1999
Published in hardback as *To Kill and Kill Again* in 2002
Published in hardback as *The Wicked Mr Hall* in 2011
This edition published in 2015

ISBN: 978 1 85782 683 8

British Library Cataloguing-in-Publication Data:

A catalogue record for this book is available from the British Library.

Design by www.envydesign.co.uk

Printed in Great Britain by CPI Group (UK) Ltd

1 3 5 7 9 10 8 6 4 2

Papers used by Publishing are natural, recyclable products made from wood
grown in sustainable forests. The manufacturing processes conform to the
environmental regulations of the country of origin.

Every attempt has been made to contact the relevant copyright-holders, but some were
unobtainable. We would be grateful if the appropriate people could contact us.

CONTENTS

INTRODUCTION

My home is a top security prison twelve miles north of York. I have been here in HMP Full Sutton for the last twenty years. I will never be released. The last thing I will see will be the green-painted walls of a prison cell. I am now seventy-eight years old.

I have been called many things — 'The Monster Butler', 'The Butler Who Served Death', 'The Ladies' Man'. In truth I am none of these things. I am Roy Hall. Before I die I want to tell my story.

Roy Archibald Hall

1

AN EASY DECISION
TO MAKE

I have been a criminal all my life. At my peak, I was possibly the best jewel thief in Britain. My record for stealing jewels would stand with anyone's. I have lived in some of the most beautiful homes imaginable. I have stayed in the best hotels, drunk the best wines and eaten the very best cuisine. But where is the life of luxury now? Now I look forward to the release of death.

I was born on 17 July 1924 in Glasgow, Scotland. My family lived in a terraced house at 15 Albert Road, Victoria Park, a poor working-class district in the west section of the city. Life was very hard in those days and poverty was all around us.

My earliest memories are of my mother dressing me for school – I must have been five or six and it would have been around 1930. Kneeling down in front of me she would vigorously rub Brylcreem into my hair before brushing it backwards to keep it out of my eyes. Putting my arms in first, she would pull on my green school blazer with the gold braid edging. Then, in a ritual that was intimate but distasteful, she would wet her handkerchief and wipe away smudges of food from around my mouth. My mother, Marian, was a beautiful, spirited woman and we would remain close all of our lives.

In over fifty years of being in and out of prison I have met many criminals. Some were illiterate, or semi-literate, but crime was one of the few ways that they could make decent money. This was not the case for me. I enjoyed school and did well at my lessons – if I had wanted to, I could have succeeded in business. As a decent scholar, my schooldays passed by without incident. I rarely got into trouble, and my parents and teachers were pleased with my progress.

I met Anne Philips when I was fifteen. She owned the newsagent's shop opposite our house, and she and my mother became friends. Anne was an elegant and attractive divorcee in her early thirties.

I started doing odd jobs for her in the shop – moving heavy stock, serving behind the counter. As the months went by, we became firm friends. I always thought of her in a special way – she had a slim figure, nice legs accentuated by high heels, and when she was close I was always aware of her perfume. At first we just made eye contact. She would catch me staring at her, but instead of just dismissing it, she looked back. That 'look' was like heaven, it excited me like nothing else. I would stand close to her whenever I got the chance and I noticed that when I did, she didn't move away. Just the opposite, in fact, she would lean into me as we talked. Talking was irrelevant, just an excuse to stand close together – so close that our bodies were almost touching and we were both aware of the energy.

It was on my sixteenth birthday, July 1940, ten months after the start of the Second World War, that the looking and leaning became something else. Anne took me out for a birthday dinner at an expensive Italian restaurant. She had been very attentive that day, very kind. I was wearing my first dinner jacket, which she had bought for me earlier. During the meal she smiled and touched my hand at any opportunity. She had the devil in her that night and was openly flirting with me. Between the first and second courses she dropped her napkin into my lap. As she retrieved it, her hand massaged my genitals and for a second she 'held' me. Finishing that meal is one of the most uncomfortable things I have ever had to do. That 'touch' had broken down all barriers and later that night she took me into her bedroom, and into her bed. I'd had sex with girlfriends of my own age, but they were young, and I was young, and it was mainly a rushed, fumbling affair. Rushed and fumbling was not what an experienced woman like Anne wanted, nor was it, in the end, what she got. She encouraged me: 'Take your time Archie, slow down, that's better, that's much better'. Before anything else, Anne would ask me to stroke her, kiss her, caress her. There was not one part of her body that did not feel my touch and my kiss. My friendly shopkeeper taught me how to please her, and ultimately how to please myself. I always

3

felt that it was she who guided me through that rocky passage from boyhood to man.

The next day, when I went home resplendent in my new dinner jacket, there was an almighty row. My father was a religious man, a member of the Scottish Presbyterian Church and, although he didn't suspect anything untoward about me staying the night in Anne's flat, he did see something wrong in my taking gifts from a divorcee twice my age. He insisted I take the jacket back. I was not to have it, people would talk. My mother thought I should keep it, what did it matter who gave it to me? We all argued. I insisted I was going to keep it, my father and neighbours could say what they liked. I remember that he was shouting in my face: as long as I lived under his roof, I would abide by his rules. Although not a fighter, I was never a 'soft' person. If my temper was 'up', people were better off leaving me be. In the midst of all the shouting, I must have picked up a kitchen knife. I know that I did, because one second I was standing there, my father shouting, and the next he had backed off. I had moved forward and the knife was held up against his face, I said to him: 'I will keep it.' After that he and I never argued; I kept the jacket and he never said boo to me again.

The thing about Anne was that she enjoyed life, she didn't exist on the measly food rations that everyone else seemed to. She ate in expensive restaurants, she dressed in nice clothes. The war hardly seemed to touch her. Now that I was her lover, I also became her dining companion.

She taught me which knives to use, which spoons to

use. I was always asking questions, eager to learn. This woman taught me so much, she was my first worldly tutor, and I wanted to be like her. I wanted a life that wasn't full of drudgery, boredom and hardship. I wanted a lifestyle like hers, only better.

As a shopkeeper Anne wasn't very diligent and she would only do her accounts when she had to. She knew her business was healthy because the shop was always busy. I discovered her secret drawer by accident. I had been in the stockroom getting her something, and as I came back into the serving area, Anne's back was to me. The till sat on the counter on top of a cloth, which overhung each side by a few inches. As I stood there, I watched her lift the cloth and open a hidden drawer and swiftly put some banknotes in. The drawer was closed in an instant, and the covering cloth put back into its previous position. At the very first opportunity, my hand was in that drawer. It was like finding a treasure trove – £10 notes, £5 notes! In those days £5 was a week's wages for a working man.

Now that I knew of the drawer, I need never be poor again – it was like having my own little bank! When I needed money, I would just take a ten, or a five pound note. Poverty was most definitely not for me. With the money that I took from the shop, I bought myself better clothes, then I started visiting restaurants on my own. I would absorb everything around me.

People with money spoke differently and had an air of confidence. I watched and learned. I became confident, too. I became careful in my speech. If you speak well,

5

people assume that you are rich. If they assume you are rich, they treat you very well.

I liked the easy money I was making, but I had left school and I needed some stimulation, something to fill my time. I didn't fancy the idea of getting some boring job earning less than I was stealing.

I didn't really make a decision, I just became a thief.

During the daytime I would walk around and look. I was always fastidious, with an eye for detail. Naturally careful and cautious, I would check everything. During the war years burglar alarms were unheard of. Entering a shop or house through a window or door was not difficult. The only danger was if the property was occupied, or if you were seen. I would always make sure that neither happened to me. I started to learn what was to become my profession.

By the time my father was conscripted into the Army, I had settled into my new way of life.

I would find a target, watch it for a few days, note when it was empty and when it wasn't and then under cover of darkness, I would rob it. In houses, I would steal only cash or small items of jewellery; in shops, cash or small items off the shelves. If I could gain entry through an unlocked door or window, I would. If at all possible I wouldn't break in. That to me seemed stupid, an obvious way of drawing attention to the theft. I became quite good at picking locks.

My mother and father were a very odd match and I wouldn't say that it was a good marriage. My father had worked for the Post Office for years, his job was to sort the mail. When I was sixteen he was forty-two. He hadn't been called up in the first batch of conscripts but, as he had military experience from the First World War, he was eventually told he must join. When his draft papers came, he left immediately for Catterick Army camp in Yorkshire.

My mother and I were to follow on as soon as we had tied up all the loose ends in Glasgow. Against my advice, and the advice of her friends, she sold our house and all its contents.

With the War now raging in Europe, there was a great deal of uncertainty in the air – none of us knew what our future might hold. German planes were blitzing all major cities and ports and I think for this reason my mother wanted the cash. After all, the house could be bombed, then we would have nothing. Packing all our personal belongings into two suitcases, we were given Army Rail Warrants, and left for Yorkshire.

Catterick was quite an exciting place to be, we were housed in the NCO Married Quarters of the camp. My father had been made a sergeant, he was kept very busy and we saw little of him. Too young to 'join up', I was offered the chance to continue my education at the camp. I turned down this offer, I had already decided how I would pass the time.

I became friendly with the Officers' batmen, who were kind of military servants. Each batman was assigned an officer to look after and their duties were to iron their charges' uniforms, polish their shoes and generally look after them and their families.

The batmen knew their officers' timetables as it was part of their job. I was just a curious young lad, so it was natural for me to ask questions. No one seemed to mind. I was careful in how I asked them though, but during the course of a conversation, I generally found out what I wanted to know – when they were in and when they were out.

Not terribly complex.

The only difference between Catterick and Glasgow was that in Catterick everyone was in uniform and it was smaller. My job stayed the same; when the officers were away I would rob them of cash and small jewels.

Unlike the location, my sex drive hadn't changed. Now that Anne Philips was too far away, I became 'friendly' with a couple of young girls on the camp. I knew now how to make love and I was always asked back for more. This wasn't much different to living in Glasgow!

It was on a day's outing to York that I became aware that my mother was having an 'affair'. I had gone to the cinema, and we had arranged to meet at a small tea shop in the city centre. As I stood and waited, a black saloon car being driven by one of the camp batmen drew up in front of me. In the back seat were Major Morris, my father's Commanding Officer, and my mother. She kissed him intimately, before stepping out of the vehicle to greet me with a smile. We had tea and neither of us discussed the Major or the kiss.

She looked wonderfully happy and that was all I cared about.

*　　　　*　　　　*

During my daytime wanderings, I would stop and chat

with all manner of soldiers and knew most of their Christian names. The War fascinated me. Would we win? Would they win? The soldiers would give me small mementoes, mostly badges, or old discharged bullet shells, sometimes these were British and sometimes German. I collected whatever I could. In my bedroom I put up a large map of Europe and, using little flags that I'd scrounged from an office clerk, I charted all the battle positions – ours and theirs. The map was no secret, the more I added to it, the prouder I was to show it off. Some of the young lads who attended the camp school would gaze at it in awe.

I had been in Catterick for several months when, one evening at about tea time, two saloon cars drew up outside the house. Eight high-ranking officers, including Major Morris, got out of the cars and knocked on our front door. They had heard stories about my bedroom. At first I thought they were looking for stolen property. This didn't worry me. Everything that I'd stolen that wasn't cash was buried in a field outside the camp fences.

The officers solemnly trudged up the stairs to my bedroom. The map on the wall was taken down, all the German and Nazi memorabilia that I'd collected was gathered up. They asked me whether I was an admirer of Hitler. I told them that I thought he had done a good job in stabilizing the German economy, but that was all!

Two days later, my father was told that he was considered too old for the Armed Forces, and was to be discharged immediately. He and his family were to leave the camp. Before 1940 had become 1941 we found ourselves back in Glasgow, and homeless.

THE WICKED MR HALL

My father returned to his job at the Post Office, and we managed to rent rooms in a large house near the University. Due to the events at the camp, I thought it best to be seen to be doing something responsible, so I became an unpaid voluntary collector for the Red Cross.

Not getting paid for trudging the streets is one thing, not making any money while trudging the streets is quite another. The first time somebody pushed paper money into the sealed collection tin, I found it easy enough to extract it and put it into my own pocket. I decided that if the Red Cross kept the coins and I kept the banknotes, this would be an arrangement suitable to both parties.

Lady Pettigrew, the administrator who had hired me, had designated me a very poor working-class area. If I wanted to get more 'paper money', something would have to change. I decided to expand my area to include the wealthier Westmuir region, and in particular, to a luxury block of flats called Kelvin Court. This block housed some of the richest people in the city and they were very generous. Soon I was collecting so much that I had to take two tins out with me. This voluntary work wasn't too bad at all – besides earning a decent wage at a job that left me my days free, I also had the added bonus of people viewing me as something of a philanthropist. Life at home settled down. My father seemed to have forgotten about his ignominious departure from the Army, and was back in the old routine at the Post Office. My mother was in the middle stages of pregnancy – a little keepsake from Major Morris, I think.

There was an old lady who had a room down the

landing from us. We rarely saw her, apart from her odd errands out to the shops. Every day she would have half-a-pint of milk delivered. I was the first to notice the collection of three or four bottles outside her door. I told my mother, and together we tried to raise her by knocking loudly on her door. Worried, my mother contacted the owner of the house who came straight round. After some consultation, it was decided that I should try and enter through her window. My bedroom was in the attic and from my window I could climb along the roof, slip the catch on one of her windows to enter her small flat, which I did. The glass on the windows was caked in grime, the flat was dingy and dark. For a few seconds I had to let my eyes adjust to the half light. When they had, I spotted a shape lying in the corner of the room. I made my way to a doorframe, and felt for a light switch. When I turned it on, I saw that the shape in the corner was the old lady lying dead in her bed.

Back outside on the landing, the owner and my mother discussed what to do. The flat had the smell of death, neither of them wanted to go in. After the old lady's body had been removed, it was decided that myself and a nurse, who also lived in the building, should search her property and see if we could discover the names and addresses of any relatives. When the nurse returned from her shift at the hospital we both entered and started the search.

The first thing we looked in was a large wooden trunk. As we opened the lid, we saw was what must have been the old woman's wedding dress. Underneath her memories of happier times, right at the bottom were two cardboard shoe boxes. Taking the tops off the boxes, we were astonished to find they were crammed full of banknotes. For seconds neither of us spoke. We just stared at the money. It was a fortune! The nurse spoke first: 'If she has relatives, they don't deserve to get this. They never bothered to visit her. She lived alone, and died alone.' I could tell she wanted to keep it. I said: 'I agree. Why don't we keep it?' Again we looked at each other. She nodded and taking a box each, we counted the money – there was one thousand pounds in each one. That was the end of my Red Cross career.

A few days later, the dead woman's only living relative came to collect her cousin's belongings. She heard about my rooftop entry, and asked me whether there was anything from the room that I'd particularly like. I'd noticed a red leather-cased travelling clock. She gave it to me. I kept that clock for years, long after I'd spent half of the old dear's life savings.

At that time in Glasgow, local people were being urged to house General Anders' army of Polish Freedom Fighters, which was stationed in Scotland. We had a spare room, and my mother agreed to a lodger. The new arrival was a Captain Jackobosky. He was a youngish man of about thirty, smart in appearance, charming and courteous. The rations that he brought into the house made him a welcome guest. I got on well with him, he had style and confidence and we shared a love of culture.

A love of culture would not be the only kind of love we would share.

My mother had put the young captain in the spare

room. He complained to her that he found the bed uncomfortable. My mother suggested that, as I slept in a double, pull-out bed-settee, he could share this with me. It happened on the first night. I was lying in bed with him when I felt his hand on my leg, then between my legs.

I had an instant erection. He told me it could be 'nice', and before I knew what was happening he was giving me a 'blow job'. I never knew that men could do that to one another, but I liked it!

Now I had the best of both worlds.

I found my new friend a charming companion and could listen to his stories for hours. He had come from a privileged background and was well travelled. In his captain's uniform, with his highly polished knee-length boots, and Slavic good looks, he seemed the epitome of European nobility. Together we would visit good restaurants and museums. In many ways he took over where Anne Philips had left off. My sexual, and cultural, education was taken one step further.

2
WHAT GOES AROUND COMES AROUND

My father wanted me to join the Post Office, but a boring nine-to-five job was not for me. I knew what I wanted. There is an excitement to stealing. The adrenalin flows and I loved the challenge and the thrill. It was an untrammelled outlet for my talents, a natural expression of my nature.

I was comfortable with, and liked, rich people and the good life. I had a lascivious appreciation of jewels and fine antiques. Just holding jewels made my cock hard. I would steal beautiful jewels from rich people. It was a conscious career decision.

I was already financially independent. I contributed towards the upkeep of the home and, when asked exactly how I spent my day, I would be vague: 'I buy and sell things, always at a profit.' My father, although not fully convinced, reluctantly accepted this job description. My mother, I think, guessed the truth, but our bond had always been closer and she would always support me.

The estate agents scam was a good one, and my own idea. Impeccably dressed, including silk gloves and hat, I would approach different offices. I would tell them that my father was serving in India in the Diplomatic Corps, and he was due to return to Scotland soon. Before his home-coming, he wanted me to find a suitable house for the family to rent. We were only interested in looking at the finest properties. As far as they were concerned I was a rich man's son, and they were very eager to please. Immediately they gave me a list of the best houses on their books, and appointments to view were quickly made.

When I went to look at the premises, the usual procedure would be a conducted tour of the house and gardens. I would show interest, the owners would invariably want to sit down over a cup of tea, and talk some more. At this point, I would mention that I would like to return with my aunt and the family solicitor to discuss contracts. A date would have to be arranged. Whichever date they said, I would suggest another. Eventually, they would innocently give me more details – they wouldn't be in that day because they had appointments or they couldn't make it on the morning of that day because they had work commitments. I would always get a definite period when I knew the house would be empty. I would already have taken note of the door locks and the type of keys used. I would return at the first possible opportunity, as arrangements can easily be changed. I always acted swiftly. If I got a chance to handle one of the outside door keys I would. These would often have a number stamped on them and if so, I would have a duplicate made – whichever way it worked, they always got robbed. My method of working remained the same; displace nothing, take only cash, small valuables or jewellery. I kept a sharp eye on local newspapers, sometimes it would be days or weeks before the victims realised they had been robbed. Besides Glasgow I also did the same thing in Edinburgh, making the forty-mile journey by train each morning, just like any other commuter.

On one occasion I was given a guided tour of a large house in the Morningside district of the city. The owner of the house was a middle-aged Jewish woman, obviously extremely wealthy. For the first time in my life I saw a marble sunken bath, I also saw a solitaire diamond ring lying on the dresser in the master bedroom. When the tour was finished we sat down to tea in the dining-room. I had been going through my usual routine about the fictitious aunt and solicitor, but my thoughts were on the diamond ring, it was one of the biggest stones I had ever seen. As the lady of the house listened, I covertly took one of my gloves and put it into my coat pocket, then standing up, declared that I must have dropped a glove somewhere. I pretended to feel through my pockets, but found nothing. Together we started to search the downstairs rooms. I watched her looking, peering hard through her glasses. I made sure that I was closest to the door that led to the hallway and stairs before saying: 'I know, I must have dropped it upstairs.' Before she could react I was bounding up the wide staircase and straight into the master bedroom where I put the ring in my pocket. I took out the missing glove, ran down the stairs holding it aloft, saying 'It's alright, I've got it'. I quickly said my goodbyes and left. Sitting in the back of a taxi I examined the ring, the stone was the size of a man's thumbnail. I ordered the taxi driver to drop me off in the city centre, and from there I walked a couple of streets to Hamilton & Ince's, a high-class jewellers.

I told the salesman that I was engaged to be married, then, taking out the ring that I said belonged to my grandmother, I asked him if he could sell me one that was similar. He told me that he didn't have one that size in stock, although he could order one for me, but did Sir realize that the cost of such a ring would be close to four thousand pounds. I now knew its value. I wouldn't sell it in Edinburgh or Glasgow, it could be traced too easily. Going home I packed my suitcase and caught the night train to London.

The next morning I went to Hatton Garden, London's jewel quarter. There I told another salesman that I'd inherited the ring from my grandmother and now I wished to sell it. He immediately went to get the manager, and together they asked me how much I wanted for it. I asked the manager what he would give me for it. After a pause, he said: 'One thousand pounds'. I shook my head: 'No, no, I've been told it's worth much more than that.' He upped his offer to one thousand two hundred and fifty. I accepted. They wrote me out a banker's draft, and a letter of introduction to their bank.

Within half an hour I had the money. I booked into a nice hotel and went shopping in London's famous West

WHAT GOES AROUND COMES AROUND

End. I had my first ever Turkish bath in Russell Square, just behind the British Museum. I loved it, it was so peaceful and left me with a feeling of cleanliness I had never known. I always loved to feel clean. I visited Soho, Mayfair and Belgravia. Twelve-hundred-and-fifty pounds was a lot of money in those days. I relaxed and became a tourist, bought my mother some nice gifts from Selfridges and treated myself to a few days of luxury.

I liked London very much. It was the centre of the nation's wealth, and theatres, museums, art galleries and Turkish baths were in abundance. The money and status were there. I knew it would only be a matter of time before I was as well. But for the moment I had presents to deliver. That evening I returned home to Glasgow.

Since starting my estate agent scam I had robbed a lot of well-to-do people. I was sure the police would have put two and two together and must now be looking for me. I decided a change of direction would be wise. An advertisement in a local newspaper provided me with a perfect alternative. The position was that of a trainee receptionist at a four-star hotel in Rothesay. I applied for and got the post. This was the perfect job for me. I watched and learned, the clientele was decidedly middle class and wealthy. I absorbed their behaviour, their collective mannerisms. Anne Philips had been a good tutor, I knew which wines went with which dishes, which cutlery to use on which occasion. I enjoyed life at the Glenburn, I had my own room, and the atmosphere was very convivial. My transformation into the perfect young gentleman was now almost complete.

THE WICKED MR HALL

On a number of occasions I had affairs with older women guests. Maybe I secrete more pheromones than the average man, but, whatever the reason, I have never had a shortage of sexual partners. These guests would invite me up to their rooms, and my sexual experience increased. Before they left the hotel they would almost always give me little gifts, by way of a thank-you. I was the 'Midnight Cowboy' thirty years before they made the film of the same name. My stay at the Glenburn was relatively short-lived – once I had learned what I wanted to know, I moved on.

*   *   *

The war in Europe was still raging. The Americans and Japanese had now joined in, and it became a global conflict. I felt that I, too, should do something. Living back with my parents I applied to join the Merchant Navy. The Merchant was helping to keep the food lines open and their ships were under constant attack from German U boats, which hoped to starve the British into submission. The Training School was near Charing Cross in Glasgow, and that was my next stop. I was keen on the idea of the Navy – the thought of travel excited me, and I would be 'doing my bit'. I had been there only a week when, for no apparent reason, I was told that I could not continue. No explanation was given. I suspected that it was connected with the incident at Catterick and I had been labelled 'subversive'. They left me no option, I went back to burglary. If they wouldn't give me a suitable job, then I would create my own. I robbed houses all over the city.

I tended to be a bit of a lone wolf socially, and it was around this period when I took to dining at the Central Station Hotel in the evenings. I would normally have a couple of drinks at the bar, then sit down to a nice meal and drinks in the restaurant. One evening while having pre-dinner drinks, I caught the eye of a well-dressed Jewish man in his mid-forties. Walking over to me, he asked me whether I'd like a drink. He looked at me in the same way as Jackoboski had, we drank and chatted for a while. When he asked me my name I told him it was Roy, Roy Fontaine. I didn't know it then but this name would stay with me for the rest of my adult life. My cultured Jewish friend said that his name was Vic and he was staying in the hotel. He invited me to be his guest at dinner and I accepted, as he interested me. Afterwards we went up to his suite, which was very, very nice. I knew he must be wealthy. We went to bed. Although he was older than me he was sexually submissive. I think we both enjoyed it.

I knew little about Vic Oliver on that first meeting, except we were both bisexual and attracted to each other. True, he would lick my balls, but is that really knowing someone? Subsequently I learned that he was a well-known entertainer, a violinist/comedian with his own radio show.

I attended many parties in the company of Vic. In 1942, 'gay' meant joyful abandonment. The parties we attended weren't given any title, but were almost exclusively male. I remember one in particular, which was held in Ivor Novello's luxury flat overlooking Piccadilly Circus. The flat was huge – polished wooden floors, scattered rugs, and in one corner a white grand piano.

Good-looking young men acted as waiters. The more mature men were the cream of London society. They would undress the serving boys with their eyes, and the serving boys would linger and coyly reciprocate. It was understood that for gifts and 'tips', the young waiters would give 'favours' to the celebrated guests.

Crotches and bottoms would be fondled openly. These were beautifully decadent occasions. Everybody present was safe in the knowledge that discretion was of paramount importance. If these people were 'outed', their careers would be ruined. But, then again, these were powerful people.

Vic would point out 'who's who' to me. Among the guests were Lord Louis Mountbatten, the writer Beverly Baxter and the playwright Terence Rattigan. As 'connections' were made, you would see couples drift off. Getting into the toilets could be a lengthy business. You would hear bouncing bedsprings behind the locked bedroom doors as you waited in the hallway. Novello was a broadminded host. People like this needed somewhere safe. With the glittering lights of the West End blacked out beneath them, the rich and famous buggered their beautiful young men.

Terence Rattigan took quite an interest in me, and I in him. He was a very handsome, very charming and talented man. While Rattigan chatted me up, Ivor Novello gave an impromptu performance on his white grand piano. I was part of a private audience being entertained by a showbusiness legend. My preference was definitely for men. Sparkling conversation, the smell of male sex, successful, powerful people – I thought I had died and gone to heaven.

Archie Hall, the working-class boy from Glasgow, belonged in the past. Not one person in that room knew a thing about my previous life. I had turned the corner. I was in the most elevated company possible, and I was accepted as a well-bred young gentleman. Not only did they accept me, the famous playwright opposite wanted to make love to me. This was the *crème de la crème*! And I was Roy Fontaine.

A few years later my male lover, Vic Oliver, became the son-in-law of the great Winston Churchill. What the great man would have thought of his son-in-law if he had known of his propensity for loitering around gents' toilets, I dread to think.

3

RICH PICKINGS

Living the life that I led on my short breaks in London provided its own opportunities. On one occasion, after coming out of the Turkish baths in Jermyn Steet, I stood on the steps and hailed a taxi. A well-dressed man a few years older than myself appeared next to me just as my cab drew up. He asked me where I was going, and whether he might share the taxi? His destination was Belgrave Mews, mine Knightsbridge. I agreed, and we both climbed in. On the journey I could feel his eyes on me, I could now recognize a gay 'come on' at twenty feet. As he got out of the car, he asked me whether I'd like to come inside for drinks – I accepted. We drank and chatted for a while. The window to his neighbours' flat was opposite his own bedroom window, with a gap of only a few feet in between. I steered the conversation on to the close proximity of the two homes. Eager to please me, he told me all about his neighbours, rich people, very quiet, no trouble at all. They were keen theatre-goers, and he was to be their guest at the opening night of a forthcoming West End show.

As the drinks went down, the eye contact and his real intentions became more evident. He went through to the bedroom and after a minute, he called me. He was lying naked, face down on the bed. In his hand was a bushel of twigs, not unlike a witch's broom. He asked me to beat him with them. Lifting my arm, I started to thrash him. Sado-masochism does nothing for me, I find it crazy. The man on the bed obviously didn't – he kept screaming 'Harder, harder'. I beat him until my arm was tired, quickly had sex with him, then left. On the way out I noted the types of locks on his door.

When 'the man who liked to be spanked with twigs' was attending the opening night of London's latest musical, I entered his flat. Exiting through his bedroom window I climbed along the roof, crossed from his building to the neighbours via a parapet on the adjoining wall. I entered his neighbours house through a bedroom window, and robbed them – a most satisfactory evening.

On my return to Glasgow I pondered new ways to make a living. The estate agents scam had run its course and was now too dangerous. I had a bit of capital and, after some deliberation, decided to open a second-hand shop. I found suitable premises in Ibrox. My mother was keen on my suggestion that she become manageress, and I set about visiting markets and auctions buying cheap stock.

At one auction, I made the acquaintance of a small,

dapper, middle-aged woman. I could see by her clothes and jewellery that she had class. Her name was Esther Henry. I had heard of her before, she was rumoured to be friends with Edward the VII's mother, old Queen Mary, and she owned Edinburgh's most prestigious antique shop. We chatted for a while and I flirted and flattered her. I knew she was rich. I gave my name as Roy Salvernon, and hinted that my family were involved in shipping. As I had hoped, she gave me her card and invited me to visit her shop. I smiled at her and told her I most definitely would pay her a visit. I didn't know on that first meeting that our association would go on for many years. Robbing Esther would eventually give me my first taste of notoriety.

Soon the shop in Ibrox was up and running, all clothes were laundered, ironed, and hung on rails. The bric-à-brac was cleaned, polished and nicely displayed. Trade flourished immediately. Within a few months I had acquired the lease of the empty shop next door, which gave me two windows to display my wares and trade increased again. Because of long-nurtured criminal contacts, goods that would not be taken to most shops would end up on my counter, with young thieves asking for a cheap price. I took full advantage of being on 'the other side of the fence', so to speak. By the time I celebrated my twenty-first birthday, I was a successful, legitimate businessman.

A young Jewish doctor came into the shop one day to sell me some odds and ends. We were of a similar type, and within days were socialising together. He would give me the names and addresses of former patients who had recently died, and it was on his advice that I started visiting bereaved families. When people are in a state of grief their business acumen suffers considerably. I would make an astute offer for the deceased's belongings. With the air of a professional mourner, I would urge their relatives to get rid of all sad memories. The money that I gave them could be spent on the living. Many useful acquisitions were gained in this way, and the stock of my shop continued to rise.

My sexual appetite has always been voracious. My doctor friend was homosexual and he introduced me to Benzedrine, an amphetamine that would keep me awake for hours on end. With seemingly endless energy I would make love to him all night long. Madame Vogely was a friend of the doctor's and soon became a friend of mine. Even allowing for my sexual excesses, my association with the Vogely family still stands out in my memory. The Madame was in her fifties, her daughter twenty-one, and her son nineteen. In one twenty-four hour period, I 'serviced' the mother during the night. Then the next morning, after she had left the house to go shopping, her daughter, who brought me breakfast in bed, enquired whether or not I liked only older women. I told her to get in beside me and see. She did and by the time she got out she knew the answer. After her departure I showered and, wearing only a bathrobe, started to shave. The nineteen-year-old son then entered the room, and while I finished shaving he went on his knees and took me in his mouth. The Vogelys were very much a 'family affair'.

In spite of the continued success of the shop, it began to feel like a millstone round my neck. The day-to-day running of it was left more and more to my mother. Occasionally I would rob somewhere just to keep my hand in. Crime and sex made me feel alive. An ordinary job, even if it was my own business, just left me feeling trapped.

Every few weeks I would travel south, and enjoy London's gay scene. I eventually got it together with Terence Rattigan. To have a man whom the Queen would eventually knight willingly go on his knees before you is a good feeling. I slept with the people society gossip columns wrote about. Today, sitting alone in my prison cell, it gives me pleasure to think about it. It is good to remember that my life hasn't always been as empty as it is now.

It wasn't often that customers came into the shop and invited me to rob them, but the Shorts stand out in my memory for doing just that. True, they didn't actually invite me to steal their belongings but, to a man like myself, if someone fairly wealthy lets you know that they will have a room full of silver gifts, and they tell you where they will be at a certain time on a certain date, they might as well have asked me to take it. The Shorts were a well-known theatrical couple, the parents of Jimmy Logan, a well-known Scottish comedian of the time, and Annie Ross the jazz singer. They also had a daughter Ella, who had emigrated to America and become a Broadway star. Ella would send her parents fur coats and other luxurious items, which were easier to obtain in America than here. What Mrs Short had no use for, she would sell to me. She became a regular customer and, as her twenty-fifth wedding anniversary loomed, she told me and my mother what a grand affair it was going to be. She gave me the time and place of the party, which was to be held in one of Glasgow's finest hotels. On the evening of the celebration, I broke into their house and stole all the anniversary gifts. The twenty-fifth is traditionally 'silver', and I was quite sure that a couple like the Shorts would indeed be given only genuine silver gifts. One of the mementoes that I stole was a solid silver cigarette case given to them by Sir Harry Lauder, who gave the world the caricature of a Scotsman being a kiltwearing, drunken skinflint carrying a wobbly walking stick. The Shorts continued to patronise the shop, and I was never questioned or suspected of being the thief.

During the summer of 1945 the War ended. Everybody, myself included, was in high spirits. I decided to close the shop, and celebrated by going to Perth and robbing a large house. Among the items I stole that day were a jade and diamond necklace and earrings. Jade was unknown to me, I had never robbed it before. Guessing that these two pieces were valuable I decided to sell them in London. I bought my usual first-class rail ticket and headed south.

The two assistants in Benson & Co seemed unsure about what to do and the elder of the pair disappeared into the manager's office. As the seconds ticked by I became more and more uneasy. My instincts were now on edge and I felt I should leave, but they had my jewels. I had come a long way to leave empty-handed. A well-dressed man wearing a bowler hat came in, and walked straight into the manager's office. I had been a thief for six years and during that time I had learned not to panic and never to flap. But distinguishing between panic and following your intuition can be a fine line. My instincts said leave, cut your losses.

RICH PICKINGS

My experience said stay cool, don't leave without the jewels or money. That day I paid the price for not listening to my inner voice – I would have twelve months in the hellhole that is Barlinie to rue that decision.

The bowler-hatted gent was the first to emerge from the office. He came straight over to me and told me he was a police officer from West End Central. He asked for ID and I tried to give him a story. He stared at me impassively. My one fear, the fear that dogs every criminal, was coming true right before my eyes. I was cornered by the police. There is an old saying 'What goes around, comes around'. I knew that the circle of my early life was then complete.

My next seven days were spent in a prison cell in Wormwood Scrubs. My parents made the four hundred-mile journey to visit me. When I appeared at Marlborough Street Magistrates Court, the Prosecutor told the Judge that he was offering no evidence in this case, as two Scottish police officers were waiting to re-arrest me. At seven o'clock that evening the two plain clothes detectives ushered me into a reserved compartment of the London to Glasgow train leaving from Euston Station. This was my first 'pinch', I had no criminal record yet. The detectives viewed me as a young criminal unlikely to be trouble to them. Showing me the handcuffs, they asked me whether I was going to behave myself. I assured them I would. As a boy in Glasgow I had heard many frightening tales of Barlinie, and my brief taste of the Scrubs had done nothing to allay my fears. I had encountered a menacing and brutal atmosphere, previously unknown to me. With each mile my dread increased.

I asked to go to the toilet just as the train was pulling into Carlisle. The Scottish border country loomed. From inside the small loo I could see the shapes of bodies boarding the train. When you are in a stressful situation, your only solace is in stolen quiet moments when you pray for strength or release. I stood in the toilet and for a few minutes I breathed deeply and wished I could relive the last few days. I cursed myself for not running from that shop, I cursed myself for taking that fateful journey south a week ago.

When I stepped out of the toilet, Carlisle station was receding into the distance and the train pushed forward into the black northern night. My two captors were standing further down the corridor, we were separated by busy luggage-laden passengers anxious for seating and rest. I must have been in a daze, because it wasn't until I saw the panic in the eyes of the detectives at our enforced separation that the possible significance of the moment hit me. My attention and theirs was on the two middle-aged women who stood between us. Their suitcases prevented me from stepping towards them, or them towards me. To this day I cannot remember having a clear thought that I would jump. But that is what I did. I felt the cold night air and the fear of the unknown as I threw open the door and leapt into the freezing void. The thrust propelled me forward and down, the ground was soft and wet. I lay face down on the earth, my heart was beating so loudly it was difficult to hear the train. I was listening for the screech of brakes and the shouting voices that would mean the chase. I lifted my head to separate the pounding of my heart from the rhythmic thunder of the train wheels. I dared not stand. I fought to control my breathing. In what seemed like an eternity, but in reality was just seconds I realised the roll of metal on metal was becoming more distant. The train continued its journey. I was free.

4

AT HER MAJESTY'S PLEASURE

After climbing up an embankment and over an advertisement hoarding, I found myself penniless on a deserted street in the Carlisle suburbs. I have a good sense of direction and, facing north, I started up a slow jog. There were ninety-six miles between my home city and the ground that my feet were pounding. Now I was really on the run. I ran on in the dark for hour after hour. Exhausted, I slept briefly in the doorway of a village church. The bitter cold and hunger made any further rest impossible, so I continued to run.

As daybreak dawned, the loneliness of that long bitter night receded. With the relief of daylight came the danger of recognition. I wanted to get myself off the open road as quickly as possible. There was little traffic, but each vehicle that passed filled me with a sense of dread. Would this one be a police car? South of Glasgow are the coal-mining fields of Lanarkshire. Workers from all over the border regions were picked up by pit buses and transported to the fields to start their early morning shifts. It was such a bus that rattled down the northern road on which I was walking. Waving frantically, I stopped it. The driver was a gnarled old man, who had probably once earned his wages underground in the same way as his passengers.

A well-dressed, if bedraggled young man must have seemed a strange sight in the early morning light. I told him that my car had been stolen north of Carlisle, that I had walked for most of the night and was desperate to get to Glasgow to report the theft. All of my money had been in the car. With a terse generosity he motioned his head to one side, a non-verbal communication that allowed me to board the lumbering but warm bus.

Knowing that my parents' house was out of bounds, I headed for the home of a criminal friend. I lay low to contemplate my situation. I knew that my mother must be anxious, so I sent a message through my friend telling her that I was in good health and close by. Against my judgement, she was adamant that she must see me. After a few days I reluctantly agreed. We organised a journey involving buses, trams and the subway. If she became suspicious of anyone or anything, she was to abandon the meeting and return home. I waited in a shop doorway some yards from where the bus dropped her off. I scanned the faces and people around her. All seemed well. As my mother approached, I stepped out of the doorway. Together we started the short walk to my refuge. I noticed the strangers immediately standing almost opposite my safe house. One was considerably older than the other, an odd pairing to a criminal that could mean police. Still walking casually, my arm linked with my mother's, I kept my eyes on the strangers. The young one crossed the road and walked swiftly in our direction. I saw, in the quick glance he threw us, that he had observed both our faces. His quick stride took him past us, I listened for some change in his footsteps. Apart from distancing, none came. For the briefest moment I felt that we were safe. Then, the older man slowly crossed the road. I felt my mother's grip on my arm tighten. Gradually we approached each other. I knew in my heart that with my mother beside me I could not run. If I did she would be arrested, taken to the station, questioned and maybe held. The professionally dressed, middle-aged man was now almost upon us. Without staring I sensed his movements. The first thing I knew about the man behind me was his hand on my shoulder. In the same instant, the older man in front of us grasped my mother's arm and identified himself and his colleague as police.

British justice stinks! My mother was a forty-four-year-old woman with a young child to care for, she had never been in trouble with the police in her life and her only crime was maternal protectiveness. The presiding judge sentenced her to twenty-eight days in 'Duke Street', Glasgow's Women's Prison. I was sentenced to eighteen months. I won't say that I didn't mind being sentenced, because I did, but I could accept that this was the natural course of things. I was a criminal. My mother was not.

Barlinie was one of Britain's toughest prisons and the

worst that Glasgow had to offer was behind its bars. The warders were brutal. Groups of them would dish out beatings for the smallest contravention of any one of the many rules. I was young and vulnerable. I kept my head down, kept myself to myself and I learned the lessons of prison life. I served that first sentence unobtrusively and quietly. I don't make moves unless I'm sure of my ground. It is part of my nature and inherent in most survivors. After serving two-thirds of my sentence I was released, but not rehabilitated. The twelve months spent inside the walls of Barlinie had been my second schooling.

Glasgow no longer suited my tastes, the pickings in London were that much richer. The day after my release I caught the night train south. I drank in Soho, a fascinating area. The bars and cafés were frequented by socialites, theatre people, artists, thieves and gangsters. It was uniquely Bohemian and that was to my taste!

I tried calling Vic Oliver a few times, but he had moved on. Que sera! I visited some old haunts. At one in Belgravia, I bumped into Terence Rattigan. It must have been two years since I'd last seen him. He was still writing hit plays. It was nice to see him and, from the way he acted, it was obvious he was pleased to see me. We chatted and had a couple of shots of brandy. He lived close by, and had only popped out to replenish drinks. He told me that he was giving a dinner party. I jokingly suggested he should have hired me to 'wait' on his table. I told him of my time at the Glenburn Hotel, that I was very good at such things and had natural talent.

The tone of the conversation changed. He became

serious, whispering his comments. Would I accompany him home? He wanted me to do something special. Would I serve his guests? He would make it worth my while. The thing was, he wanted me to serve after-dinner port with a difference. He wanted me to do it in the nude. I was to approach the dining table with everything hanging out. He wanted me to titillate his friends.

I have few inhibitions. I would make money and useful contacts. Later I might rob them, who knew what might happen? Before the end of the evening, I was sure my ball bag would be empty. I agreed.

After swallowing our brandies, we walked the short distance back to his flat. It was spacious and luxurious. God knows how much he was earning. He had a small kitchen staff of two waiters and a cook. I was told to wait in the kitchen until the appointed time. I had undressed and was wearing only a bathrobe. While I waited, I drank brandy at the kitchen table.

When my cue came, the cook slid the bathrobe from my shoulders and placed a tray with a decanter full of port in my hands. I entered. For a naked body the temperature was not warm, and my penis was not at its most glorious. In fact, because of the chill and my nerves, it was limp and bloodless, a shadow of its usual self. I approached the table and as I poured the first glass, I felt a hand cup my balls and give them a loving squeeze. With each glass that I filled, different hands caressed me. The blood streamed into my cock – you could have hung your hat on it. Rattigan's dining-room was mirrored wall to wall. The men who weren't looking at me directly were staring into the mirror. Hands slid up and down my body. The fingers of the rich and privileged probed my arse and I smiled and served. This beat leaning up against a bar daydreaming. As they touched me, I wondered who I'd be able to rob, and who I wouldn't.

I was open to everything and, in time, everything would happen to me. This was just another day.

I took a flat in central London and, as the many commuters travelled into the city to work, I travelled to the suburbs that they had just emptied and robbed them. I had been leading the city life for just under a year, when I was arrested on a burglary charge. I asked for fifty other offences to be taken into consideration, and was sentenced to two years. I was taken to HMP Wandsworth, in South West London. In Wandsworth, I met many people who would remain lifelong friends. In Wandsworth I met John Wooton.

In 1948 prison time was hard time. You were not allowed to speak to a warder unless he addressed you first. You had one bath a week in five inches of tepid water, you dried yourself with a piece of coarse canvas cloth. At night you sat in your cold, dank cell sewing mailbags. The bags secreted a black, sticky resin, which would eventually cover your hands.

It was no place for the faint-hearted. All my life I had abhorred violence. Although no victim, I was not a natural fighter. Words were my weapons. During exercise one day, my Scottish accent attracted the attention of a big English con. Taller, heavier and older than me, he decided he wanted to fight me – his reason being that he didn't like the way I spoke. In prison, if you can avoid using your slop-out pot, you do. As the exercise period was finishing, I took my chance to use the toilet. The English con followed me. His intent was clear and, barging into me, he raised his fists. The voice of John Wooton prevented that first punch being thrown. He said, 'Why don't you try me? I'm more your size.' Aged 34, Wooton was ten years my senior. He was tall with dark hair and an athletic build. In his youth he had done some boxing and he 'shaped up' to the would-be bully. This man had wanted a soft target, someone to beat, someone to take his anger out on. He left the toilet without saying a word. He never bothered me again. For John and myself, it was the start of a friendship that would shape both our lives. Years later, this most trusted friend would marry my mother, making him my official stepfather.

Wooton and myself were cut from the same cloth. Neither of us was typical of our backgrounds. We both moved easily in middle- and upper-class circles. John was no more a typical Londoner than I was a typical Glaswegian. We would work together, but in 1948 our time had not yet come. Before Wooton would come Johnny Collins. Collins was an East End thief, two years older than myself. Now he was a typical cockney – he loved going to the dogs, gambling, womanising, and boozing. On his right cheek he bore a scar, which he said was inflicted by Jack Spot, the so-called King of the Underworld who preceded the Kray twins as possibly the most feared man in London. Collins release date was some months before mine and close to Christmas. Before he left he made a promise to see me alright for 25 December. Although difficult to escape from, the prisons of post-war Britain were nothing like the security-conscious places they are today. There was no barbed wire on top of the walls, nothing was alarmed, there were no perimeter fences. If you could somehow scale the walls, you could quite feasibly get to the exterior doors and windows of the prison itself. There was a glassless, but barred, window to the tailoring shop. Stacked next to the bars were rolls of cheap cloth, which were used for prison uniforms. On the day before his release, Johnny pulled me to one side and told me of his proposal. On one of the days leading up to Christmas Eve, he would scale the walls, cross the wasteground and, reaching inside the bars of the tailor shop window, he would leave me some Christmas cheer to share with our mutual friends.

As the time approached I would deftly slip my hands in between the rolls of material to see whether he had been as good as his word. There was nothing on the twenty-first, nothing on the twenty-second or twenty-third. As Christmas Eve dawned, my hopes were fading fast. Many men make promises on the inside only to regain their liberty and adopt an 'out of sight, out of mind' policy. I considered Johnny's to be just one more empty promise. But at 11.30 that morning, as I slipped my hand between the rolls of cloth, my fingers touched a package. The last hand that touched that package had been Johnny Collins'. He had come through. His word was good.

Later he would tell me how he and a friend had borrowed a builder's open-backed van. They had an extended ladder, blankets and torches. Together they scaled the wall, flipping the heavy wooden ladder over from one side to the other. The friend stayed with the ladder and carried a torch to guide Collins back to him. Taking the bag of presents Johnny crossed the wasteland, then sticking close to the wall, made his way to the tailoring shop window.

That night in our cell, a small group of us sat around the open package. He had left us cigarettes, tins of fruit, salmon, biscuits and two bottles of the finest Scotch whisky. Jack Spot had allegedly seen fit to put a razor to Collins' face, but that Christmas Eve five smiling cons raised their tin mugs to the East End villain, who was probably the world's most unlikely Santa Claus.

I have many memories of that first Wandsworth sentence. Chirpy Downes was another Eastender, his cousin Terry Downes was a famous boxer of the time. We were in the prison chapel one Sunday morning when the Chaplain delivering his sermon said: 'When I was a child, I spoke as a child, and acted as a child.' With his head bowed, Chirpy said: 'You still are a child.' It wasn't said in a loud voice, it was just a disgruntled con letting slip a sarcastic remark. As we filed out of the chapel at the end of the service, a screw stopped Chirpy in his tracks. He told him he was putting him on punishment for insolence. Chirpy grabbed hold of him and a fight ensued. Later that evening a group of warders with batons entered Chirpy's cell and beat him badly. He was taken to the punishment block where he was put in solitary on rations of bread and water. After a few days, he was taken to the prison laundry. There waiting for him were twelve warders and the prison doctor. He was forced to take off his shirt and, after having a wide leather belt fastened around his waist to protect his kidneys, he was strapped to a large timber triangle. Out of his vision, one of the warders was handed the 'cat o' nine tails'. Chirpy would never know which prison officer beat him. The 'cat' is a barbaric flogging implement. It has a short handle from which hang nine strips of knotted leather. After each lash, the prison doctor would check the prisoner's heartbeat. The 'Cat' would strip the skin from a man's back. On top of the beating, flogging, solitary, bread and water and loss of wages, Chirpy lost remission time, increasing the length of his sentence.

The experience of prison hardens a man, providing justification for the crimes he is going to commit.

5
CLIMBING THE CRIMINAL LADDER

I was moved to Pentonville to finish my sentence. By the time I was released, 1948 had given way to 1949, and winter had given way to summer. It was on a bright sunny morning that I walked away from north London's notorious debtors' prison. I was a free man again. There were a number of vehicles parked in the street outside the gates. One was a black taxi cab. I passed by without giving it a second thought, for the moment all I wanted to experience was the sense of freedom. As I passed the cab, the back door was thrown open and a voice that I recognised called me: 'Morning Roy, want a lift?'. The voice belonged to Johnny Collins. We drove to Billingsgate market where the pubs were open early to cater for the market traders. We had some drinks, then went for a large cooked breakfast. From there we booked into the Great Eastern Hotel in Paddington. In the hotel room, I took off the clothes that I had worn as I walked away from the prison, and threw them away. This was a ritual I would observe after every sentence. After luxuriating in a hot bath to wash away the prison stench, Johnny told me of his plan. For professional villains, smash-and-grab raids on jewellers were becoming fashionable. Our smash-and-grab team would consist of three men. The 'driver', Dave Perry – a man who could do almost anything with a car; the 'smasher', Collins himself, whose job was to break the large plate-glass windows, without injuring us with falling glass or knocking the jewellery pads out of reach; and the 'grabber', someone with a knowledge of jewellery who could select what should be taken and take it. I was to be the final man in Collins' team. I was climbing the criminal ladder.

The first jewellery shop to have their window display rearranged by Messrs Collins, Hall and Perry was the London Goldsmith Co. on Cricklewood Broadway. Dave Perry parked the car, engine running, level with the window. We had already decided earlier in the day what we were going to take. Johnny claw hammered the window at all the right points and the shattering pieces of glass dropped well away from the pads I wanted. The evening pedestrians just stood and stared, as if watching a scene from a gangster movie.

Johnny, hammer in hand, kept a watchful eye on the staring public. Remaining calm and focused, I lifted the pads of jewellery that we wanted and dropped them into a small bag, then we both stepped back into the car. Perry, engine at full throttle, sped off into the London night. Sitting alone in the back seat, I took the jewels out of the display pads and wrapped them in handkerchiefs. Perry, having taken a series of turns in back streets, dropped me off at a designated point. From there I would either take a tube or pick up a waiting vehicle. There was a publican at the Raven in the City of London who acted as our fence. I went directly to him and upstairs away from nosey drinkers, we did our business. The jewels became money and the money was split three ways. Over the next two years, jewellers all over the city and suburbs would be visited by us. The three of us lived the high life – we worked when we wanted and we spent as much as we wanted.

We had separate social lives – Dave lived in Paddington and was a family man; Johnny, whose family all lived around the Cable street area of the East End was a home boy, spending his time at the dog tracks, gambling houses and pubs of the East End. My tastes were a touch more cultured – Turkish baths in the city, first-class hotel bars, theatres and museums. I lived the life of a well-heeled city gent.

A petty criminal from West London, finding himself in a tight spot with the Old Bill, gave information on an aquaintance of his. It was our misfortune that the acquaintance was Dave Perry, our driver. Hours before we were due to go on our latest raid, Perry was nicked and held for questioning at Paddington Green.

Johnny and I were uneasy about the situation. We were sure that Dave could be trusted but, even so, it was risky to do anything local. On a whim, I told Johnny about a single-windowed jewellers in Buchanan Street, Glasgow. That afternoon we drove north. We checked the surrounding area for a suitable escape route. Buchanan Street was patrolled during the night hours by a mounted policeman wielding a long riot stick. To park outside the shop would undoubtedly attract his attention and was out of the question. After some thought, we decided to park in an adjacent street. There was a warehouse door that, if we could gain access, would give us a short cut from Buchanan Street to our parked car. After playing with the lock, we gained entry. The door leading to our car was unlocked and ready. Both doors were small entrance doors, housed within the much larger warehouse doors – far too small for a man on horseback to follow. We watched and waited. The mounted patrolman ambled from one street to the other rhythmically tapping the hard, dark stick on his highly polished riding boot. We watched him time and time again. We noticed that not once did he turn around and look behind him. The only noise was the echo of the horse's hooves on the concrete and the almost indiscernible tap of stick upon boot. As he neared the end of the street, we quietly moved into position. On this occasion for speed's sake, we would both smash and both grab. The horse was as far away from us as possible and we prepared for action. I took two folded canvas bags from my pocket and laid them on the ground, Collins took out two claw hammers, one from each pocket. With hammers raised, we listened to the clatter of the horse's hooves in the clear night. As the animal reached the end of the street we struck. Our hammers hit the glass in unison, the blows were deliberate and precise. The window fell away. At the other end of the street, the once ambling equine member of the Glasgow police force was being jockeyed into a gallop. On its back, stick swinging, voice screaming, a red-faced Glaswegian police officer bore down upon us. Our hands grabbed the jewels in a controlled frenzy, we took everything. With hammers still in our hands, we ran for our freedom. With each step we took, the sound of the hooves and the screams of the patrolman grew ever nearer. We hit the warehouse door on a skid, changing direction from north to east in a lurch of our bodies, motivated by pure fear. As we bundled through the small door, I could hear the snorts of air blasting from the horse's nostrils.

Tired but elated, we began the four-hundred-mile journey back to London. We drove through the night, taking turns, one sleeping, one driving. By daybreak we were back in the capital. Collins and I were quite a team. We took thousands, and we took it from right under people's noses. I have never 'grassed' in my life, and when villains turn Queen's evidence on other villains, it makes me nauseous. Before we had time fully to savour our triumph in the Buchanan Street dash, I was paid a visit by the police. At the same time, in the East End, Collins was also picked up. Information had been given. Some low life criminal we had been stupid enough to confide in had given us up. So much for honour among thieves.

I got three years and Johnny, being older, got four. It was back to Wandsworth. On my last sentence I had been treated as an ordinary category prisoner. Now, my leap from the train had been added to my file and I was regarded as an escape risk. The last time I had been in prison, the E men (escape risk prisoners) had smallish yellow patches on their blue trouser legs. The yellow patches had increased in size, almost covering the whole leg. One blue leg, one yellow leg – I looked like a clown!

I have always accepted what I am – I am a criminal. I'm not a sex case, I don't rape people or interfere with children, I am a professional thief. I had always been good and, with the passage of time, would get even better. I believe in dignity. If my professional 'calling' is outside the law, then so be it. Loss of liberty and privacy were prices I accepted I had to pay. However, being made to look foolish was completely unacceptable.

On my very first time out on exercise I took off those ridiculous trousers and threw them with all my might over the prison wall. Immediately, I was grabbed by warders and marched in front of the Governor. I was told in no uncertain terms that I would comply with regulations. I nodded in tacit agreement. The next day while out on exercise I did the same thing. This time other cons followed my lead. A dozen pairs of yellow and blue trousers landed on the free streets of south-west London. Let the public see what the Home Office was expecting us to wear.

There was now some tension between the E men and prison staff. We were confined to our cells and, come the next morning, more of the same – no exercise, no work details. We sat in our cells, wondering what the penal system had in store for us. Just before noon the next day a dozen of us were taken down to reception. John

Wooton was one of the number. We were transferred to Winchester.

The atmosphere there was considerably easier. We were again put into patches, but this time the old smaller ones. Something that irked me about this E business, was that I had never actually escaped from a prison. I had absconded from police custody while on a train, but this was a completely different matter to escaping from a secure prison. I pleaded my case with the Governor. Eventually he relented. I was taken off the E list and reverted to an ordinary category prisoner. I went to work as a painter. When I wasn't working, I would spend many hours reading about jewellery, porcelains and antiques. For the first time I read a book about being 'In Service' – butlering, to be precise. As prison time goes, this was quite an easy sentence. I got my full remission, and was released in the spring of 1952.

6

LIFESTYLES OF THE
RICH AND INFAMOUS

Back in Glasgow things were changing. My parents' marriage had never been that good, but now the cracks were beginning to show. It was never mentioned, but I often wondered whether my father ever noticed that his young son Donald was the spitting image of his old Army CO. For a few weeks I just rested and enjoyed eating palatable food again. Occasionally I burgled somewhere just to stop myself getting rusty. I continued to visit Esther Henry's antique shop. It was now several years since we had first met and she had only ever known me as Roy Salvernon. Still, I had her trust. I always made sure I had a packet of black Sobrini cigarettes on me, her favourite brand. An ornate tin box stood on the floor of her office, which was locked in a glass cabinet at night. I had never managed to see its contents, but it intrigued me.

As the summer approached, my parents' marriage finally

disintegrated. My mother applied for and got the position of live-in housekeeper to a Mrs Dunsmuir of Kilbride Castle, Dunblane, Perthshire. As it had been her decision to leave my father, she did not feel that she could deprive him of his home as well. After giving her time to settle in, I paid her a visit. Mrs Dunsmuir was *nouveau riche*, an ordinary girl from the nearby town who had married a rich American. On his death, she had returned to Scotland as the Grand Dame. As well as my mother, she employed a young Swedish *au pair*. At Mrs Dunsmuir's invitation I stayed as my mother's guest. To relieve the boredom I started carrying out small tasks, helping to serve dinner and suchlike. The lady of the castle deemed me competent and I was offered a job on her staff – helping around the house and chauffeuring her when needed. The duties were light and easy, the surroundings pleasant. Within days I had noted the items of true value and where they were kept. The other thing that caught my eye was Agnetha, the young Swedish *au pair*.

Back in Winchester, I had given John Wooton my parents' Glasgow address and, with directions from my father, my old prison friend turned up at the castle. He couldn't have timed it better, it was a beautiful sunny day, and employer and staff were enjoying food and drinks on the lawn. John turned on the charm, and Mrs Dunsmuir took an immediate shine to the London-born criminal. If she had known that her staff was now resembling a Wandsworth old boys' reunion party, she would have had a heart attack.

Agnetha was a young girl looking for fun. Stuck out in

the Scottish countryside, miles from any nightlife, she was desperate for some stimulation. I charmed her, I slept with her, I liked her. After my time in prison, she was a welcome diversion. There seemed to be an immediate bond between John and my mother, she had a level of intimacy with him that I had never witnessed between her and my father. Increasingly her off-duty hours were spent with him. I spent mine with Agnetha. Since puberty my sexual drive has been a strong controlling factor in my life. In the morning I awake with a hard on, and when I lay my head on my pillow at night, it is generally with a hard on. I was hard, on the Saturday morning that I walked into Mrs Dunsmuir's bedroom, to see Agnetha stretching over the mattress making the mistress's bed. I took her from behind, she liked me to take control. Neither of us bothered to undress, her knickers were just moved to one side as I entered her. Her favourite position was 'doggy'. Her face was buried in the floral eiderdown. There was no sound to make me turn. But I did anyway. Our employer was standing framed in the doorway. She told me that she wanted me off her staff, and off her property... immediately. Wiping and putting away my now flaccid cock, I said, 'Certainly, Madam. If you will give me a cheque in lieu of a month's wages, I will be on my way.' At this, we argued, but when she realised that I would not give way, she grudgingly paid me my severance money. Much to my delight, Agnetha packed her suitcase and followed me out of the castle. I said my goodbyes to John and my mother and Agnetha and I lounged and lusted away two weeks in Jersey.

Being a thief, I had many criminal contacts. I knew some of the best forgers in the business. For a price, I obtained new references and a new past. I scoured top people's magazines for new employment. Working for someone is better than just robbing them on a whim. You get to enjoy all the creature comforts, you have time to assess what it is that you'll take and, if you have the right contacts, replacements can be made. Most people don't know a good fake from the real thing. Also, I enjoyed nobility, it was something I had a feel for.

The Warren-Connells were as far removed from Mrs Dunsmuir as a warm puppy is from a hot dog. They were 'old money', part of a long-established, Clydeside shipping family. They were now in retirement at their stately mansion, Park Hall. They were a pleasure to work for. They had true class. Mrs Warren-Connell was a bubbly vivacious woman, with Christian values that she actually practised as well as preached. Her husband was an utterly charming elder statesman of industry.

The staff that I joined consisted of three gardeners, a gamekeeper, chauffeur, cook/housekeeper and two maids. I worked diligently and hard. Within a short while I won the trust of my new employers. As the height of the holiday season approached, all staff, along with the Warren-Connells themselves, left for a two-week break. The responsibility for running the house was mine.

I had been alone in the house for a few days when, one morning, an envelope among the mail caught my eye. It was larger the the rest of the post, edged with gold braid and, on the back was the crest of St James's Palace. I wanted to know what was inside, so I steamed it open. It read: 'I am commanded by Her Majesty the Queen to invite you to a Royal Garden Party at the Palace of Holyrood House, Edinburgh.'

The 'you' in the invitation, of course referred to Mr Warren-Connell. Holyrood House is the Queen's official Edinburgh residence. In the past I had been a guest of Her Majesty on a number of occasions, none of them enjoyable. This would help to redress the balance.

On the morning of the party, wearing a hired morning suit and driving the family Bentley, I quietly slipped out of Park Hall. I took care to make sure that none of the gardeners saw me. Looking every inch an upper class gent, I drove to Edinburgh to meet the Queen. After checking the guest list and then studying my invitation, a uniformed policeman saluted me and waved me through the gates to the Palace. The party was a grand affair. No sticky black resin oozing from mailbags for these guests of Her Majesty. Instead, it was paper-thin cucumber sandwiches, the finest teas, and Police Commissioners and Judges strolling around the lawns. *En route* to the Palace I had popped into Esther Henry's antique shop. I presented her with a dozen red roses and casually mentioned where I was going. She was most impressed. Esther herself had royal connections. In her eyes my credibility was now beyond reproach. After the garden party, I retired to a first-class hotel and drank some brandy. It was obvious to the management where I'd been. They would remember my face and if I ever needed to cash a dud cheque or work another con they would be most receptive. A good thief continually lays groundwork. I have always considered myself to be a professional person.

A couple of days later I was sunbathing in the garden when an unmarked car came down the drive. Two men got out. I didn't need to be told they were police. They asked me the whereabouts of Roy Fontaine. I hadn't committed any real crime since my arrival. Impersonating my employer at a royal garden party was hardly likely to get me sent to prison. I said that I was Fontaine. They asked me what I wanted in that area, why was I there? I told them I was tired of London and tired of prison. I wanted to build a new life for myself. I wanted to go straight.

They questioned me about a robbery at an egg packing station, where a safe had been blown. I said: 'Look at my file, I've got absolutely no experience with safes.' They questioned me about other robberies. For each one I had an alibi. I was clean. Before they left they wished me good luck.

Two days later at seven o'clock in the evening, just before dinner was due to be served, the phone rang in the hallway. I picked it up. At the exact same second in her upstairs bedroom, Mrs Warren-Connell also lifted the receiver. I remained silent and listened. A man's voice at the other end of the line identified himself as a detective with the local CID. He asked the lady of the house whether she realised that her butler was a jewel thief with a prison record. I heard her gasp in astonishment. 'Do you think he has come here to rob us?'. 'Well, I don't think he's taken the job for the good of his health' was the reply. She asked whether I was wanted by the police. To this he had to answer no. 'But,' he carried on, 'I have a map in front of me on my wall, and all I can see are danger points. I'd be much happier if he wasn't in my area.' By now I had the voice – it belonged to one of the detectives who had visited me, the one who'd wished me good luck. I waited for Mrs Warren-Connell to replace the receiver. Slowly I put mine down, too. It was time to think.

The Warren-Connells came downstairs, and I went about my duties of serving their evening meal. There was a certain tension evident. It was Mrs Warren-Connell who spoke, as I was serving them their after-dinner drinks, 'Roy, have you ever been in trouble with the police?' Shamefacedly, I admitted that I had. It had been in London a long time ago. I had fallen in with bad company and had paid the price of being sent to prison. I bitterly regretted it. I was now happy in my work and with my life. I wished that my past could remain just that, my past. Mrs Warren-Connell's Christian goodness gushed to the surface. She told me of the phone call she had received and then asked the most direct question of the evening: 'Roy, have you come here to rob us?' 'Certainly not madam. Never,' I replied. Her face softened: 'I have talked this over with my husband and we both agree that everyone should be given a second chance. If I were to dismiss you, and you returned to London and once more got into trouble, I would never be able to look my maker in the face. We wish you to continue working for us.' I thanked them both and left the room. I still had my job, but I had been scuppered.

My next move was made up for me. I was walking in the grounds of the estate when I overheard a conversation between one of the gardeners and the gamekeeper. 'Tam, the village bobby, has asked me to keep an eye on him,' said the gardener. 'He's a notorious thief, I don't know why the mistress just doesn't throw him out.' Villagers gossip, that is a fact of life and soon everyone would know of my past. I was in an impossible situation. Any local criminal could take advantage of me being here. If anything went missing, I would be prime suspect. Of course my hands were now tied and any ideas I had of replacing precious jewels with fakes was very risky. I knew that I had to leave. I explained my situation to the Warren-Connells. They both seemed upset and were very gracious. I was given three months' salary and Mrs Warren-Connell, again displaying her generosity of spirit, phoned around her friends, eventually finding me a position at a shooting lodge miles from anywhere in the Highlands. I thanked them but, not wishing to isolate myself, I turned down the post. That day I returned to London.

John and my mother had become an item. They had left the castle, and set up home in a flat in Paddington. It was there that I told John of my plan to visit Esther Henry, and of the black tin box that stood in her office. We decided that, if we could, we would rob it.

There was a public telephone box opposite Esther's shop. Inside the shop were two phones, one at the front near the window, and one in the office at the rear. The plan, which was simplicity itself, was this: I would enter the shop, engage her in conversation and steer her to the front of the shop. John would be watching from the phone box. He would call and Esther would answer on the phone near the window. Pretending to be an American businessman interested in buying Georgian silver, he would keep her diverted and I would go into the office. I would be carrying a briefcase, containing three telephone directories. I would unlock the box using the keys that were hanging on a hook on the wall. The contents of the box would be emptied into the briefcase, the telephone directories placed in the box for weight. I would lock the box and keep the keys. As soon as I had the goodies, I would make my excuses and leave the shop. If successful, I would remove my hat as I walked out of the door. John would get into the car and fire the engine, then we would get out of Edinburgh as quickly as possible.

The plan that I had formulated was exactly how it happened. Esther smiled at me as I left. I told her I had an appointment and would call back later. I had taken the precaution of booking myself a rail ticket from Carlisle to London. On the drive from Edinburgh to the English border, John and I would split the haul. I would do the second half of the journey by train and John would continue by road. If one of us was caught, we would still have half the haul. I had no real expectations as to what the box contained – just a feeling that it would be worthwhile. As we sat in the car dividing up the contents, neither of us knew that we had just committed Scotland's biggest ever jewel robbery. The year was 1953.

We had jewels of every description, plus American and Canadian dollars. I reached London slightly before John. In the early hours of the morning we started to assess what our prize was worth. We estimated a market value of somewhere around £100,000, a fortune. Early the next morning John went to Fleet Street to check the Scottish papers for reports of the robbery. Nothing. I went to my buyer with one hundred and twenty pieces of jewellery for him to look at. We bargained, I knew his style. At one point I stood up and offered to take the jewels abroad, where I would get the sum I wanted. The price went up, and up, and up. It reached £40,000. I phoned John and told him the figure. We decided to accept. Cut of the one hundred and twenty pieces, the fence bought eighty. We still had another £10,000 in foreign currency, and forty pieces of difficult to move but still valuable jewellery. We had hit the jackpot.

Back in Edinburgh, Louis Henry, Esther's adult son, put the locked black tin box back into the glass cabinet where it was stored at night. He noticed that the keys were not in their usual place, and he assumed his mother must have them on her. It wasn't until the start of the next business day that they both realised the keys were actually missing. An ironmonger was summoned to the shop to break open the locked box. When the lid was removed the Henrys found themselves looking at three neatly piled telephone directories. The alarm was raised. Esther Henry was friendly with half the crowned heads of Europe as well as Governnment ministers, and at least one Chief Constable of the Scottish police force. I realised that once she and the police had put two and two together, every police force in Britain would be after me. I would now become top priority. Wooton was a known criminal associate of mine, his name would soon come into the frame. We thought it best to disappear. Loaded with money, and posing as American businessmen, we headed for the south coast for a short holiday.

Torquay is a charming seaside resort. John and I booked ourselves into a first-class hotel under assumed names. On that first evening, the main ballroom was host to a fundraising charity auction and dinner. We both mingled with the other guests, then with some brandies inside us we entered into the spirit of things. John bid £30 for a basket of fruit, which he promptly gave back to the waiter and told him to re-auction. This won a round of applause from the crowd. I successfully bid for two bottles of champagne, which I didn't re-auction but instead had sent over to the Mayor's table as a gift from two foreign businessmen. Within minutes we were invited to join the local dignitaries. Later that evening, I had drinks and conversation with the Chief Constable of Devon and Cornwall. We both remarked how obvious criminals were – little did he know, I was probably the country's most wanted thief. The next day we were invited to the Mayor's chambers for sherry. Our pictures had been taken by the local papers. At that moment we had Torquay in the palm of our hands. We could have presented dud cheques to any jewellers in town, and they would have been accepted without question.

Feeling isolated in London, my mother came down to join us. She and John took some time out and did all the usual tourist stuff – horse-drawn carriage rides and walks on the beach. That was the week of the Grand National.

THE WICKED MR HALL

With plenty of money and in ebullient mood, I fancied a flutter. I was standing on my hotel balcony early one morning. In the distance was a small boy in a rowing boat. He looked so tiny – the mist almost shrouded him completely. I looked through the racing pages, there were horses running in that week's Aintree meeting called 'Sailing Light' and 'Early Mist'. I bet one hundred pounds each way in a double. To my delight they both won. I won thousands, thousands that I did not need. I was on a roll, this was a life worth living.

Ten years older than me, John was now considering settling down. My mother and he were thinking along the lines of a pub or guest house. Torquay was a possible option and the idea of retiring to the coast seemed to be on the cards. A life of active crime was now becoming a thing of the past for John. He was reaching mid-life and he had my mother to think of. We looked at what was left of the haul from Edinburgh – forty pieces of jewellery, which contained some aquamarines thought by *The Guardian* to be part of the Hungarian crown jewels. I paid John a fair price for his share. He was now cut free from the job, all he had to do was keep out of the reach of the long arm of the law.

While John and my mother started looking at possible properties, I took a quick trip to London's East End. Carrying a suitcase of clothes that I didn't really need, I knocked on the door of Johnny Collins. There was no need for long-winded explantions. I handed him the case, told him that, as a security measure, I was dispersing my belongings among a few trusted friends. I asked him to put it in his attic and told him that I would be back to claim it some day. Among the thieves I worked with, there was a code of honour. None of us would break it, it was our bond, our only security in a world full of law-abiding grasses.

My mother and John rented a furnished house in Margate. It was from there John called me and said he had something he wanted me to look at. Criminals are averse to discussing things in detail over the phone. I didn't ask any questions but drove straight to the coast. As I got out of my brand-new Jaguar, outside John's door, I noticed a man reading a newspaper on a park bench. He gave me more than a passing glance. My instincts immediately went on alert. Entering the house I told John of my suspicions. He said I was imagining it, but I was growing uneasier by the second. I told him I was leaving, whatever it was he wanted to discuss would have to wait. Going straight back out, I got into the Jag and fired the engine. The man on the park bench had disappeared. I couldn't clarify my thoughts. All I knew was that I smelled danger. I drove around the corner and two police cars came at me from either side. A third, as if from nowhere, appeared behind me. Plain clothes and uniforms surrounded my car. I was nicked.

This was the price I paid for not wanting to leave my new car. If I had left by the back door, jumped over some garden fences and made my way on foot, maybe I would have got away. But I didn't. The car was my pride and joy. They say material greed is one of man's downfalls – on that day it was mine.

I denied everything. Under heavy escort, we were all taken first to London and then on to Edinburgh by train. We arrived late at night. The train and platform emptied before anyone moved. When we stepped off the train we were met by Chief Constable Merrilees. Coming up to me he shook my hand and said: 'So you're Fontaine. Well, I'm glad it was one of her own – and not foreigners like the press have been speculating.

Prior to us robbing her, Esther Henry had been on something of a shopping expedition. She had travelled through Europe buying antiques and jewels. Her eventual destination was Egypt where she had been invited by the late King Farouk to look at some *objets d'art* that he was willing to sell. After making her purchases she had returned to Scotland via Hungary, where I think she bought the aquamarines now in my possession. Theories had been put forward by the Scottish press that she had been trailed back to Edinburgh by a gang of international jewel thieves, who robbed her.

We were offered a deal. If we pleaded guilty, they would say that we had stolen less than we had. Also, John would be charged only with receiving stolen property. I was against doing any deal with the police. My mind was changed for me by my mother – she was their lever. If we agreed to the deal, she would not be charged. If we didn't she would stand alongside us in the dock as an accessory. I had already caused her to be imprisoned once and it was not something I wished to repeat. I agreed to their terms. At Edinburgh Crown Court, I received three years and John, four. My mother walked free.

7

HALCYON DAYS

My first sentence at Barlinie had been quite an ordeal. I was young and vulnerable and the place had terrified me. I had now done the rounds a bit and prison was just an occupational hazard. This term would be different from most, our faces had been all over the newspapers and we were described as 'gentlemen thieves'. We had carried out what was at that time Scotland's biggest ever jewel robbery. The cons all wanted to shake our hands and the warders were friendly. I had taken another step up the criminal ladder. Due to the publicity that the robbery and trial had attracted, we both expected to be transferred to Peterhead – Scotland's most secure and toughest prison. In due time we were informed that this would indeed be the case. I was in the exercise yard one day, when the Chief Officer, along with the prison Chaplain, both came over to see me. They told me a vacancy had come up in the prison library. If I wanted the job it was mine, and it meant I could stay at Barlinie. When I had first done time in an English prison, John had looked after me. In Scottish prisons, the English are viewed with some suspicion. John knew no one north of the border, so now was the time for me to look after him. Like shit to a blanket, partners should stick together. But it was a quandary. The librarians' jobs are much sought after – they give you freedom of movement and it is possible to get involved in all kind of scams. There's no doubt that this was a golden opportunity for me to do the easiest time possible. I was given a few days to make up my mind. That evening in our cell John and I talked it through. He said I would be a fool to turn it down. He could cope with Peterhead, he would be alright. I agreed, but I had reservations. Those reservations proved to be unfounded, as within days of his arrival at his new prison he was given the librarian's job as well. My mother rented a cottage at more or less equal distances from both prisons and visited us both regularly. It was a tough time for her.

For different reasons it was a tough time for Esther Henry who also visited me on numerous occasions. She wanted her jewels back and wanted to know whether I had sold them or still had them. I wasn't saying anything. A visit gets you out of your cell. Visitors buy you coffee and give you cigarettes. On the inside you do what you have to do.

Even in prison Esther proved to be useful. As long as she thought there was a chance of recovering her precious jewels, she would play along with whatever I wanted. As

Christmas approached, the convicts' concert was in preparation. A few prisoners had got a band together but were short of a drum kit. Esther had connections on the prison board of governors. The band got its drum kit, a decent one, on hire from one of Glasgow's music stores.

The library job proved to be everything that I'd hoped it would be. Within weeks, I was involved in every possible fiddle. I got to know a young warder who was kind to me in many ways. As we got to know each other, he started to confide in me. His relations with his wife were not all that he wanted and he craved extra spice. Could I get him porn? He didn't dare buy it on the outside for fear of discovery. We set up a trade. I would get him the porn if he would get me tobacco, which was in those days still the main prison currency. For me one trade led to another, it gave me an interest, something to do.

It was no secret that I smoked, but no one but me knew of the young warder's sexual inclinations. Gradually the dynamics of our relationship changed. I knew his secret, it was in his interests to keep me happy. Hanging still took place in British prisons and at that time there was a man in Barlinie awaiting execution. For reasons I didn't really understand, I wanted to see the death cell. No con ever saw this and if you did you never got a chance to tell the tale. I pestered the warder for days and eventually, when no other cons or warders were around, he unlocked the door and I stepped inside. I realised immediately that if we could get a photograph, the tabloid press would pay thousands for it. I pressed the idea, tried to persuade him that if we used a third party, no one need ever know we had instigated it. He baulked at this, because if found out, he would lose his job and be prosecuted under the Official Secrets Act. I stopped pestering him about the photo and satisfied my curiosity by walking around the cell. To call it a cell was not an adequate description. It consisted of three levels – the top of the gallows where the rope and pulley system were, the trap door where the prisoner stands with a bag on his head and rope around his neck, and the sandpit below where, with his neck stretched, he would dangle. Standing on the trap door and looking through the hatch in the ceiling to the top of the gallows, I said: 'Who'd be a murderer and risk finding himself standing here?' I didn't know then that if it hadn't been for the Abolitionists that is exactly where I would have later stood. Maybe subconsciously, we know things about ourselves that we'd rather not.

As I approached the end of my sentence, I was transferred to Duke Street women's prison. This was where, years ago, my mother had lived for a month. Now it had all but been closed down and most of the inmates had been moved to a modern new jail in Greenock. There was now just a skeleton staff and a few prisoners, whose duties were to pack up all stores and sundries before the old prison was consigned to the pages of history. I was assigned to work under the Steward. My duties were to parcel up and label remaining stores and to clean the Steward's office every morning. The Governor's office was next to the office I cleaned. It was cleaned by one of the female prisoners. The bolts that locked it were on her side. We became friendly. If we were caught fraternising it would mean the punishment block and time added onto our sentences so we had to exercise the utmost care. Once the offices had been cleaned, any rubbish or ashes had to be emptied at the rubbish tip. Before she would make this walk, my friend would tap on the door. She would start her walk to the huge dustbins and a minute later I would follow. There, among the piles of garbage and industrial-sized bins, we would grab each other. Using the bins as cover, we would lean against the cold metal and fuck. For both of us, those few minutes would be the only happiness that the day contained. We would walk back to prison life separately one minute apart. Such is the life of convicts.

*   *   *

It was 6.00am on a cold winter morning in 1955 when I stepped free, back on to the Glasgow streets of my childhood. I visited a few friends, and picked up some initial moving about money. Then, after buying a dozen red roses, I caught the train to Edinburgh. When I walked through the front door of Esther's shop, the cleaning lady started giving me verbal abuse: 'How dare you show your face here? How could you betray your friendship with Esther?' I just smiled and, walking over to Esther, gave her the roses. The lady from whom I'd robbed a fortune smiled back. Esther had class. She still wanted to buy back her jewels. She asked me whether that was possible and I said: 'Esther, you are an immensely wealthy woman. Enjoy the rest of your life.' With that I left. I never saw her again. In

1961 she was killed in a plane crash in Brazil. The cleaning woman had it wrong, I hadn't betrayed my friendship with Esther, she had always been a 'mark'. She was wealthy and I was a thief, but we truly had liked each other.

From the shop, I went straight to the Caledonian Railway Station and caught the first train to London. Back on what was now my home ground, I made my way to Cable Street in the East End. I knocked on the front door of Johnny Collins' flat. He was pleased to see me and we had some drinks. The suitcase that I had left with him had never been opened. Honour. It wasn't until I was back in my hotel room that I opened it. There was one particular suit that I was interested in, one particular suit jacket. I felt underneath the collar. Right at the back, at the nape point, my fingers found what they were looking for. Sellotaped there was a small key. The next morning that same small key opened up a safety deposit box in Harrods' bank. I looked at my immediate future, the jewels that were before my eyes would have made a certain Scottish shopkeeper the happiest woman alive. The well-connected Ms Henry still had plenty of everything. Me, I had to start again, and this was my beginning.

I rented a flat in Knightsbridge and employed a young guy to keep it clean, press my suits, and so on. I started to look round and figure out my next move. A chance meeting in a pub in Windsor brought it about. I was sitting in the bar drinking expensive brandy and luxuriating in my freedom. Only those who have known imprisonment truly appreciate freedom. There was a young attractive woman, sitting alone at a table near me. I thought I might like to fuck her; if not, maybe have some enjoyable conversation. I smiled at her and asked her whether she would like a drink. She accepted and joined me. During the conversation, all thoughts of fucking her vanished. What she was telling me meant business. She knew of a publican in Slough, who was a silent partner in a bookmaking business. This young woman had once worked for him as a barmaid. Slowly, plying her all the time with drinks, I coaxed the information I wanted out of her. The publican was rich and he and his wife were heavy drinkers. In the cellar, among the beer barrels, was a safe. All large denomination banknotes went to that safe along with his wife's jewellery. I left the drunken girl in the pub. The less she knew about me the better. Instead, I flew to Edinburgh. On the flight back to London there were two of us. The man with me was Ambrose Carr, a safeblower, one of the best. We took rooms in a lodging-house in Slough. Every day we watched the pub, the Montague Arms. For three weeks, we observed all their habits, all their routines.

The broadcaster Gilbert Harding was a regular at the bar. He was a gay man, very famous in his day. I became good friends with him and his lover, a director of a well-known international company. These were wealthy, well-connected men. These friendships, as with Esther Henry, were purely superficial. I was on the lookout for useful information. If I had sex, well, that was a bonus.

I have never been frightened of dogs. The pub dog was a Great Dane, which was allowed to roam around the bar and was popular with the customers. It was especially friendly with me, although I was probably the only customer in the pub who was secretly feeding it fresh raw meat from my pocket. That dog just loved me in no time. When we had seen enough, we decided to make our move. We chose a night when both the landlord and landlady were almost legless at closing time. They wouldn't so much sleep as collapse. We waited until 3.00am before entering. The Great Dane was on us in seconds and, just as quickly, it was eating its favourite raw meat and following my hand as I led it into the back yard, down the path and into a shed, where it sat with a bag full of steak. I locked the door. After Ambrose had done his stuff, we covered the safe in coats, cushions, beer towels, rugs, everything. It must have been the warmest safe in the south of England. When Ambrose's gelignite exploded, it became the hottest. I went into the yard and looked up at the publicans' bedroom window. No lights went on, they were so pissed they'd have slept through a nuclear explosion. However, when the smoke had cleared, we saw that the safe door had buckled, but it was jammed. Ambrose said all that was needed was a touch of 'jelly' on the hinges. He did his work. Again, we covered the safe, and bang! This explosion was not so loud. The safe door, falling on to the stone cellar floor made more noise. The safe was full of banknotes, in a corner at the back were some nice pieces of jewellery. I was back in business.

In our lodging rooms, we showered and shampooed. All the clothes that we had worn were put into rubbish bags and disposed of. If we were caught, the police forensics would have nothing. We counted the money – there was

£29,000. For a cheap price, I bought Ambrose's share of the jewels. He caught the first plane back to Edinburgh, and I returned to my London flat. It felt good to be working again.

8

A TOUCH OF CLASS

Chatting to young girls in pubs can be very gainful for a man such as myself. A young *au pair* in the Maidenhead area, in a repeat of the Slough episode, told me one evening of her rich employers in Henley, who were leaving for the USA in a few days and were taking all their valuables with them. That morning, the lady of the house had taken her jewellery taken out of her bank safe deposit box, and it was now locked in a travelling wardrobe trunk. Before she got too drunk, the *au pair* gave me the address. The next day, in a hired car on a bent licence, I drove past my next target.

It was a nice property, a modern lodge house. I parked the car in the lane and approached their drive. There were no cars parked there. I walked up to the front door and rang the bell. No answer. I walked round to the back of the house and quickly entered. I started with the master

77

bedroom and found some trinkets, but nothing of real value. I methodically searched all the rooms, including the travelling wardrobe trunk.

In the dining-room, in a glass case, there was a beautiful piece of Renaissance work – a Spanish galleon with portholes of rubies and diamonds encrusted in its bows. It was beautiful, I took it.

On a whim, I drove to Scotland. I approached Louis Henry, Esther's son. I showed him the galleon. He offered me £2,000. I refused, as that was a fraction of its value. I put the galleon in a safe place and considered spending a couple of days in Edinburgh visiting old friends. I was in my hotel room getting changed when there was a knock at the door. Opening it, I was confronted by four policemen. The one who did all the talking was an old acquaintance, Chief Constable Merrilees. He had been speaking to Louis Henry. His men searched the room, but found nothing. They took me down the station and interrogated me for four hours. Being questioned by the police, like going to prison, is all part of my professional work. I've never given them anything. In the end, lacking evidence they released me. Going to Louis had been cheeky, but I couldn't resist it. I had a night out in Edinburgh, but I felt a nagging sense of frustration. I was sure the information the *au pair* had given me on the jewels had been genuine. The next day, back in Henley, I watched the lodge house. Packing boxes were now evident at all the windows. There was movement. By mid-morning the man had left in his car and, just before lunchtime, I watched his wife and the young *au pair*, along with the children, get into a family estate car and drive off. I waited a few minutes and then approached. I went in through the same set of French windows. This time there was less to search, as most of the belongings were in packing crates, presumably for storage. I felt behind the folds in the gathered curtains that framed the Georgian windows. I looked in food tins. I used all the tricks I had learned during my many prison terms. The airing cupboard was the last place I looked. In between the folded blankets, I found the jewel case. I had just earned myself another few thousand pounds.

I was under no pressure to sell, because I still had plenty of money. I took my latest little earner to Harrods, where I deposited it in my safety deposit box. Afterwards, I went to what is essentially the store's own pub, the Green Man Bar. I was in a good mood, I was free, earning money hand over fist and enjoying the thrill and excitement of being a good thief. All I wanted now, besides the brandies that were giving me a nice warm glow, was sex. Either gender would do. As the brandies slid down my throat, I looked around the bar. They were met, and held, by a well-groomed, quite handsome, middle-aged man. We looked at each other, both knowing, or hopefully knowing, what the other wanted. He raised his glass and, using body language, signalled would I care to join him for a drink. I walked over. After the initial ritual, he asked me whether I'd like to go to his flat for drinks. I said yes. We ended up in bed together.

He was a nice man, a brilliant conversationalist. This was hardly surprising, for he was Bob Boothby, later to be made a Lord and one of Europe's most noted political speakers.

He was a close friend of Harold and Dorothy MacMillan and was rumoured to have been Dorothy's lover. This could well be true, there were photographs of her in his bedroom. There were also photographs of the Kray twins. Again, it was alleged that he and Ronnie had been lovers. Boothby had been private secretary and friend to Winston Churchill. His photograph was next to one of Ronnie Kray, which seemed a strange combination. The class barriers that separate us are not as strong as some people might imagine. After sex, we lay in bed and talked. I mentioned that I was thinking of taking a holiday abroad. I wanted a break from England. Bob said a friend of his had a beautiful villa in Antibes. The owner was a man called Peter Seals, Somerset Maugham's gay lover. Throughout the summer, Seals would take in selected house guests. The villa was exclusively male. After making a phone call I flew out. The Mediterranean sunshine was just what I needed. There were five luxurious bedrooms, two handsome young houseboys whose duties were more than just domestic, and three other guests. We ate delicious food, drank the finest wines, and enjoyed the young boys and each other. Some nights we went out to the Eden Rock Hotel to gamble and drink. I was on my most honest behaviour. With a lifestyle where so many other senses were being satisfied, I had no need to rob. This decadent two-week orgy perfectly suited my true sexuality and my true nature. We fitted like hand and glove. I felt like an Emperor, with drink, food and flesh at my indulgence.

I flew back to London on my own. After a few days I flew out to the Channel Islands and, staying in a nice hotel, just soaked up the sun for a week. From there I popped over to France. I have loved Paris since my youth, when Jackobosky would tell me tales of Europe's cultural capital. I visited museums and art galleries. For weeks now, my life had been one of pure pleasure. In the past, the prison time I've done has been hard and to my way of thinking, this evened things up a bit. After a decent summer break, I knew I must consider working again so I returned to London and, sitting in my Knightsbridge flat, I began to think about my next scam.

*   *   *

Bernstein's was a West End theatrical costumers that could supply you with any kind of dress imaginable. I ordered a Sheik's headdress and bought some iodine to darken my skin. In Regent Street, I purchased twelve high-quality leather suitcases. Then back at my flat, I got on the phone and started to put things into motion. I made a reservation for Sheikh Mutlak Medinah, arriving in this country from the Middle East in one week's time. My choice of hotel was important. At this stage I didn't want a top one. If suspicious, the top establishments run a security check. 'Good' hotels, however, are just pleased to get the seemingly high-class custom. For the next seven days, I bombarded the hotel with a series of bogus phone calls from Embassies and banks. Using the names of bona fide stockbrokers, I established the Sheikh's identity. The plan was to have three stages, all with the same purpose – to establish identity and credibility. On the morning of stage one, in full Arab garb, I was picked up by a hired chauffeur-driven Rolls Royce and taken to the first hotel. Bellboys were tripping over each other to carry my luggage up to my suite. I spoke hardly at all and paid for everything in cash. After a few days, via room service, I had the management book me into the Cumberland, one of London's finest, but not yet the top, hotels. The Cumberland asked no questions, the reservation had been made by another hotel manager. I did the same thing again for five days – I sat and bided my time. I tipped room service well – I was growing into my role, the way an actor does. Finally, I was ready to make my move.

I asked the management to reserve me a suite at the Dorchester, one of London's oldest and grandest establishments. By the time I walked into the Dorchester, I was a convincingly arrogant Arab oil Sheikh. This was not my first time in this hotel, there were two reasons behind choosing it as the base for the con. One was status, and the other was that I knew the layout. The suites had two points of exit. As I looked around my rooms, I thought, perfect. I couldn't afford to talk to anyone for fear of blowing my cover, so for a couple of days, I just enjoyed the luxuries of the suite and hotel.

On the third day, I called down to the manager and asked whether I might look at some jewellery. I wanted to buy some gifts for my fiancée back in Arabia. Samples from the jewellers in the hotel lobby were sent up to me. I looked at them, and was disdainful. Was this the best they could offer me? They said they could make some telephone calls. I insisted on looking only at the best. On my behalf, the management phoned up some of Hatton Garden's finest jewellers. The shops immediately dispatched assistants with attaché cases full of samples. Within a short while, these assistants were in my suite, eager to sell me their wares. Disdainfully I looked through the fine jewels, seemingly uninterested. I told them I would bathe and think about it. Once in the bathroom, I switched on all the taps. I left the door ajar. When the room was full of steam. I reached through the half-open door: 'Pass me some things to look at while I bathe.' Greedy for commission, the assistants passed me their sample cases. Standing, still fully dressed in the steam-filled room, I emptied all the sample cases into a briefcase. I slipped off the Arab robes. Underneath I was wearing a suit and tie and I looked like a Middle Eastern business-man. I left the bathroom by the suite's second exit. Walking swiftly down the staff staircase, I left the hotel through the side-door of the building. I hailed a taxi, which dropped me off in Knightsbridge. From there I walked to my flat in Hans Crescent and emptied the briefcase. I had spent a few thousand pounds setting this job up, but laying on my carpet were £300,000-worth of gems. I heard later from contacts that, at around the same time that I arrived back at my flat, six increasingly worried jewellers entered an empty steam-filled bathroom. On the floor they found the discarded clothing of an Arab Sheikh, and six empty attaché cases. To use a more modern vernacular, they had been well and truly tangoed.

My confidence was now sky high. If there was a better thief in Britain, I didn't know of him. For that matter, neither did the police. Talking of which, I was never questioned or charged with that job. The days when Collins and I smashed through plate-glass windows to relieve jewellers of their possessions now seemed far off and coarse. Now it was all about sleight of hand and confidence. I window shopped at the city's many jewellery shops. I had a good memory for settings and would study the ring and then the salesman. I had copies made through forger friends, then I would return to the shop, making sure it was a different assistant before entering. I would ask to see the ring and, quite often with the salesman or woman at my elbow, I would 'switch'. It was easy. The copies would sometimes cost hundreds of pounds, but I would walk out of the shop with a £10,000-£12,000 ring. On other occasions, an elegantly dressed woman would pose as my fiancée. She would try on an engagement ring and I would complain that the true beauty of the stone couldn't be seen in artificial light. All three of us would step on to the street. Shops were more trusting in those days. Buried under the hum of London's constant traffic, they wouldn't hear the running engine of John Wooton's car. As my fiancée looked at the stone, I would take out my cigarettes. Just as I went to light one, I would drop the lighter. In true servile deference, the assistant would bend down to pick it up. By the time he looked up, me and my pretend wife-to-be were in the car. By the time he had straightened up, lighter in hand, the three of us were losing ourselves in the city's ever busy traffic. Those were halcyon days. I was at my peak.

9

FROM ONE EXTREME TO ANOTHER

At 6.00am on 7 January 1956, the Metropolitan Police smashed through the front door of my flat in Hans Crescent, Knightsbridge. I was awake with the first thud of the sledgehammer and knew instantly what was happening. I heard the rush of feet as they gained entry. My bedroom door opened and three plain clothes detectives crowded round my bed. I could hear other officers starting a search of my flat.

'Get dressed, Fontaine, you're nicked.' I asked, 'What are the charges?'

'We are arresting you on suspicion of the robbery of the Montague Arms public house in Slough.' They cited two other jewel robberies, including the one in Henley. I dressed with an audience.

I was taken initially to Slough police station, charged then held on remand. At Buckinghamshire Quarter

Sessions, I was sentenced to ten years for each robbery and five years for a revolver they had found in the flat. The judge sentenced me to thirty-five years in prison. Luckily, the ten-year sentences were to run concurrently. That meant I would serve one ten-year stretch for the three robberies. But I was still looking at a fifteen-year sentence. This was tantamount to a life sentence in Britain. I had been done for three robberies, all without violence, all against wealthy people who were well insured. This sentence was out of all proportion to the crimes. I got five years for a gun that had never been fired or used in intimidation. This left a bitter taste in my mouth. The man before me in the dock was was a paedophile, convicted of sexually molesting fourteen young boys. He got six years. With time off, he would be back hanging around school playgrounds in four. English justice makes me sick. It is designed to protect property more than people. It is implemented by the rich. A fucking pervert who wrecks children's lives is treated more leniently than a thief.

I was taken to Wandsworth. Again. Even before I was given a cell, I was in trouble. While being examined by a doctor, I refuse to call him 'sir'. I told him I only used the term 'sir' to people, irrespective of position or class, when I have some respect for them. I had no respect for him. Within days I had been transferred to Parkhurst on the Isle of Wight. Parkhurst was Britain's very own Alcatraz. It had the worst warders, the harshest regime, and the most serious criminals. It is the very worst prison that I've been in, and I've been in plenty. I was back on the 'E' list. The only prisoners I associated with were also 'E' men. We ate together, worked together. We were segregated from the other cons and had less free time and the worst work duties. As 'escapees', we were considered to be subversives and troublemakers. They sought to break our spirit. In fact this had the opposite effect. The one saving grace of being an 'E' man, is that those that surround you are not weak, they are survivors, men the authorities have tried to break and failed. The more they tried to crush us, the more we supported each other. The more they attacked us, the stronger we grew. Together we kept our spirits up. But camaraderie or not, life was cold and grey. On bitter, dark winter nights, it was hard to feel good.

Some officers would assault you and put you on punishment for the slightest thing. In some cases you wouldn't have done anything, they would do it for you.

A favourite pastime of one of the officers was to go into a con's cell while he was on exercise. He would press live matches into the cracks in the stone floor. When you returned from exercise, he would have you pulled out of your cell and stripped naked. Everything would be searched, the cell, all your belongings, thrown about, quite often smashed. Naked, you would stand in the corridor, watching. Eventually, the matches would be found. Then, it was down to the Punishment Block to solitary confinement, bread and water, and some indiscriminate whacks from their sticks to set you on your way. Rehabilitation?

I spent a lot of time on punishment, a lot of time shivering, eating only bread, drinking only water. I was on punishment once, when the door was opened and a screw asked me whether I'd like to do a work detail with another prisoner. I accepted. We were both taken down the corridor and shown three stripped cells. We were to whitewash them. Giving us brushes and buckets of paint the warder left. He obviously thought it was safe to leave us alone. The other con and I started to work. There was a ventilator shaft in the wall of the cell. I knew the layout of the prison, as I had been there now almost two-and-a-half years. The shaft must run to the outside areas. In the corridor outside the cells was a wall cupboard. It would almost certainly be for maintenance tools. The brushes and buckets we were using would have come from that cupboard. I played with the padlock and opened it. We found a bricklayer's trowel and a steel chisel. Quickly, we removed the cover of the shaft. There was just enough room for two men to crawl inside. Clambering up the wall, both of us crawled into the dark cavity. To our amazement, the brickwork was already crumbling and we started to dig. To the left of the shaft ran two pipes, which I guessed were gas. I warned my friend not to lean on them. We crawled to a bend in the shaft. If we followed the shaft, it would just take us further into the prison. On the other side to the brickwork in front of us, would be one of the outside yards, then a wall, and then the Forest of Parkhurst, and freedom.

Frantically we stabbed at the disintegrating sand and cement round the bricks. My eyes had now adjusted to the dim light. I could see what I was doing. I tried to dig without swinging my arms. The constricted space meant our bodies were touching, our arms and elbows continually banging each other. The other con seemed to be in more of a panic than me. Twice he just missed my face with the sharp trowel. I told him to be careful, that we must dig together in unison. As I jabbed the chisel into the bricks, I knew that in as little as half an hour we could be free, or, if discovered in the ventilator shaft on an escape attempt, we could be lying naked in a cell, taking a beating. I dug and prayed, neither one less important than the other. My partner switched arms, saying his left was too tired. Now his swings were going from right to left. The first one grazed the wall and the momentum took it straight into one of the gas pipes. Gas leaked out, right beside us. I got him to hold his thumb on the leak while I slithered out of the shaft, broke into the maintenance cupboard again and got some putty. Crawling back to my friend, we plugged the leak as best we could. The escape attempt was over. The slightest movement would cause the leak to open. We had wasted precious time. Hurriedly we got out of the shaft and cleaned ourselves. We replaced the cover, put everything back as it had been. It was only when the fear of being caught for our aborted attempt had subsided that the abject desolation hit me. We had had a chance of escape, and we had failed. Our wall painting was neither enthusiastic nor thorough.

That night, with all doors locked and all the cons in bed, the putty on the gas pipe blew. Gas started to pour out through ventilator shafts throughout the prison. The sirens went up and the prison was evacuated. Hundreds of half-dressed men stood under floodlights in the exercise yard. The engineers were sent for and eventually the gas leak was traced. It was discovered that the brickwork surrounding the pipes had been freshly dug away. The atmosphere in the segregation wing was tense. I wondered whether the warder would admit to leaving two men on punishment, one an 'E' man, to work unsupervised. Time would tell. Whatever happened to the warder never became public. That they had managed to trace back the sequence of events became evident two days later, when my partner and I were both transferred off the island. He went to Chelmsford, and I went to Nottingham.

There is 'hard time', and there is just 'time'. I've never been in a prison that has been like a holiday camp, as some political right-wingers on the outside seem to think. Having your liberty taken away from you is punishment enough, no matter what the conditions. When those conditions are brutal, your life is a struggle and the very worst of you comes to the surface. Brutalise a human being, and you end up with a brutal human being. If Parkhurst brought out the worst in me, Nottingham would bring out the best. The Governor was a man called David Inders. He was popular with staff and inmates. Inders was a humanitarian, a simple enough word to say, but a tall order for a human being to meet. In the jungle that is the penal system, he was like a breath of fresh air. He was not a weak man, his actions were guided by his morals. His natural bias was to look for what was best in a man. I gave him not one moment's trouble. I fight fire with fire. If there's no fire, I don't imagine flames. Within weeks, I was taken off the 'E' list.

John and my mother, on leaving Scotland, had settled in

Stafford. Nottingham was much easier to get to than Parkhurst and every fortnight Wooton made the forty-mile journey to visit. There was a civilian, an odd-job man, who worked at the prison. I think originally he had been a gardener. In middle age he did whatever work he could get. His name was Bert and he would have his dinner in the mess alongside us. He was an unassuming, simple soul. Prisoners and staff alike treated him well. Bert would travel to work on his bicycle. He had an allotment, and often he would bring a sackful of his own vegetables into the prison to sell to the catering department. No warder ever stopped Bert, or looked in his sack.

Every fortnight after his visit John would leave, in a left luggage locker on Nottingham railway station, a bag of 'goodies' for me. During the visit, the ticket for the key was slipped into my hand. The day after John's visit, Bert would purposely sit near me during lunch. At some point during that meal, the ticket would move from my hand to his. Twenty-four hours later, just before the end of the lunch period, Bert would come into the prison mess. He would be carrying a sack of vegetables for the kitchen and on his way, he would stop and sit with me for a quick chat. The sack would be placed between us. Inside would be a carrier bag. I would take out the bag, and Bert would go on his way. During lunch time and leisure periods, cons can move around quite freely. Within minutes I would have the bag back in my cell. Inside were all the things that made life bearable – tins of salmon, a bottle of wine, good soap, razor blades, aftershave. For me, being dirty and unkempt was as difficult as losing my freedom.

The other thing that made life bearable was Whisky. Whisky was a two-month-old kitten when I first got her. Again, it was Bert I had to thank. Both John and myself made sure that Bert was well rewarded for the little favours he did us. In prison, any prison, the only side of yourself that you dare show is the hardest aspect of your character. When a con is allowed an animal or a bird, for some brief period of the day, it lets him reveal his gentler side. For a human who spends half his life in a cage, it is easy to lose yourself. Whisky went some way towards keeping me a reasonably worthwhile human being. I loved that little cat.

Besides the company, Whisky also gave me a purpose. I would scheme and trade to get fresh meat and fish for her. I never once gave her tinned food. Cats are independent animals and sometimes she would vanish for a few days. But whenever I was on exercise, I had only to whistle and, within seconds, the small ginger cat would be winding herself around my ankles. Sometimes it would be minutes before I could move. She gave me so much pleasure, too much to put a price on.

I had been at Nottingham for a few months when I was called from exercise, because the Governor wanted to see me. The way he looked at me as I stood in his office gave me an inkling of what was to come. The words were quietly spoken: 'Roy, I'm very sorry to have to tell you this. I have just been informed by a Glasgow solicitor that your father died yesterday.' The main thing I felt was shock. He asked me whether I wanted compassionate leave to attend the funeral. I said: 'Not if I have to stand by my father's coffin in handcuffs, with a policeman at each arm.' Inders looked at me. I went on: 'My father was a law-abiding lay preacher. To be at his graveside, handcuffed and under escort, would shame his memory.'

Again Inders looked at me, but this time the look was more penetrating. He held my gaze, before speaking. 'If ... IF ... I recommend you for two days unescorted compassionate leave, will you give me your word that at the end of those two days on the morning of the third day, that you will report to the main gate by 8.00am.' I nodded. Inders continued: 'If, after giving me your word, you fail me, I will give you my word that as long as I am a prison governor, I will never grant such a privilege to any other prisoner in my custody again.' This time I looked him in the eye: 'I give you my word.'

Dressed in my own clothes, I went to reception where I was given a black tie and a rail warrant. I was also given a few pounds subsistence money. The Deputy Governor drove me to the station. Dropping me off, he pushed a ten-shilling note into my hand and said: 'Have a couple of beers while you wait for the train.'

The journey north was strange. I was elated to be free, but sad for my father. Also, I knew that the freedom was an illusion. As the train rumbled northwards, two thoughts continually swam around in my head. I had no warders and no bars to restrain me. If I wanted to go on the run, I could. As my head filled with the dreams of free life, the realisation of why I was sitting on the train hit me – I would never see my father again.

I arrived in Glasgow early Monday morning and went straight to see the solicitor who was handling my father's affairs. His house and contents had been put up for sale. All proceeds were to be split equally between me and my brother Donald – nothing for my mother.

John Wooton, my mother and Donald had all travelled up from England. The funeral was a quiet affair, just family and a clerk from the solicitor's office attended. When the service was over, I was keen to put some things right. I asked the young clerk to open up my father's house, as there were some personal possessions that I didn't want sold. He hesitated, saying that it wasn't really in his authority. I pressed the issue and he gave way. I suggested to John that he take Donald for a drink, while my mother accompanied me to the house.

I kept the clerk occupied with a series of requests for various pieces of furniture to be held in store and not auctioned. While I did this, my mother moved about the house, quietly taking back personal mementoes that she had bought years before. Both of us took small items that had belonged to my father, nothing of value, just things to remind us that he had once lived, and been part of our lives.

For the rest of the day, I put death out of my mind. I spent time with John and my mother, before taking myself off to have other needs satisfied with a woman friend of mine. We ate, drank and then fucked. It was good to be held, good to feel like a human being. I caught the overnight train south. John, my mother and Donald all came to see me off. I waved goodbye to them and to my freedom. I sat on the train with a carrier bag beside me. Inside were miniature bottles of scotch, shortbread and cigarettes. I had an arrangement with a trustee who would meet me on the gate. With this little bag, I could trade. On that journey south I raged inside. The closer the train got to Nottingham, the greater my inner conflict. I knew that Inders was a decent man. I knew that I had given him my word. But, what was that? With a thief, my word was my bond. But, Inders? Decent as he was, he was still a prison official. Prison governors, prison warders, police, they were all my enemies and always had been. Their job was to catch me and imprison me. Mine was to stop that happening. We stood on opposite sides of the fence. What did it matter if I broke my word to my enemy? Where was the dishonour in that? I knew that I had enough contacts and was good enough at my job to 'go to ground'. I wasn't some petty criminal the police could find in five minutes. I could live my life, just as I had before. With fresh identity, fresh documents, how could they find me? I thought, and thought, and thought, the grind of the wheels on the track and the rhythmic sway of the carriage merging with my see sawing emotions. Would I go back, or would I run? Would I go back, or would I run? Would I go back ...?

Eventually I slept. I was woken with a jolt when the train pulled in at Crewe and some people boarded. These were free people. For them this journey was just one more ride. For me it was a journey back to grey stone walls, bars and locked doors. With each mile my turmoil increased. There was no respite. The train pulled into Nottingham at 6.40am. To me, it seemed a beautiful morning and I savoured each breath.

I had an hour and ten minutes before I was due at the

gate. If I wasn't there, the police would have an arrest warrant out on me within the hour. I strolled to the Station Hotel and ordered myself a nice breakfast. After explaining to the waiter where I was going, I got him to bring me two double brandies. With the alcohol still burning in my throat, I stood up, picked up the carrier bag and began my walk to the prison. I had decided. I would go back. I learned one thing that day. I would never again give my word to my enemy.

I pressed the bell, long and hard. The door opened and I stepped back into my caged world.

In 1963 the Home Secretary decreed that Preventative Detention Prisoners, who had not received more than a six-year remission, would now be granted full remission. When this news stopped being rumour and became fact, I opened a bottle of wine, gave Whisky some fresh fish and, at the first opportunity, phoned Harrods and gave them my measurements for a new suit. I wrote to John and my mother and told them I was getting out.

10

HIGH SOCIETY

I was released on the beautifully sunny spring day of 19 March 1963. John and my mother were both there to meet me. I was holding Whisky in a cardboard box, this was her first taste of freedom, as she had never before been outside the prison walls. For both of us it was a fresh start. It was a happy day. Freedom! We drove to Stafford.

That evening, John and my mother threw a huge party for me, mostly old friends and criminals. Stafford is not exactly central and a lot of people made long journeys. There was no doubt that, as far as criminals were concerned, I had a lot of respect. I was most definitely first division.

It was now twelve years since John and my mother had first met at Kilbride Castle. They fitted together like hand and glove. It was with pride that I gave away my mother to my best friend when they were married on the 26 March 1963. The only thing that would ever separate them was death. For me, that was one of the best days ever. John, my best friend and partner, was now officially my stepfather. We got drunk like never before.

The only thing to sour the occasion was a friend of mine – we had done time together in Winchester. He was known as the 'Thin Man'. He was a good thief, but he never should have stolen my mother's wedding present money. He dipped her purse for a few hundred quid on the morning of the ceremony. At the reception, I confronted him. He denied it, as obviously he would. I searched him in the garden. He was too clever to have anything on him. I told him to fuck off – how dare he steal from my mother? I never had proof, but I knew it was him. I never saw him again. You don't take from your own!

During my seven years in prison, life on the outside had changed – the music and fashions in particular. Now it was all The Beatles and Carnaby Street. They said the country was booming. I wondered what I would do next. What I wanted to do was to steal the jewels off the neck and fingers of the world's most glamorous movie star. My fingers touched Elizabeth Taylor's diamond rings when we shook hands. An opportunity missed, it keeps me awake at nights.

It was a chance meeting with Terence Rattigan that led me straight into the private Dorchester suite of Liz Taylor and Richard Burton. Rattigan was now middle-aged. Apart from his status he held no interest for me. The feeling wasn't reciprocated. He gazed into my eyes, pushed himself up against me whenever possible. He was a pain in the arse – which was just what he wanted from me, but I wasn't 'pitching'.

I let him talk. When he told me he was among a select few guests invited to have drinks with Hollywood's golden couple, I actually took some interest. Burton and Taylor were like showbiz royalty, the world's most charismatic and glamorous stars. Where they went, the world's press followed. My mood with Rattigan softened and I told him I would be delighted to accompany him.

They had the Oliver Messel Suite. Taylor was extravagantly beautiful and Burton looked like a screen icon. In between rubbing himself up against me, Rattigan introduced me to everyone. Sammy Davis Jnr was there, Mia Farrow, her mother Maureen O'Sullivan, and various writers, producers, and anyone else who could wangle an invitation to come and pay homage.

It was an honour to be in their company. Even so, while everyone fawned around Cleopatra, I tried all the bedroom doors. They were locked. Bastards! The people in this room were worth a fortune. As I couldn't rob them, I relaxed and enjoyed the company. I liked Richard particularly. Taylor was dripping in gold, but I couldn't get anywhere near it. Rattigan's continual rubbing up against me was getting on my nerves. Let him go and pay one of the pouting youths who hung around the lobby. I made my excuses and left.

I had always enjoyed being 'in service'. Besides living in beautiful homes that I could rob, there was also the air of class. My appreciation for antiques, beautiful jewellery and culture are separate from my criminality. Working for the rich meant that I could indulge both aspects of myself. I scoured the pages of *Tatler*, and found an appointment as companion to a rich elderly American and his wife. I travelled to Cooden Beach, Bexhill, Sussex and moved into a luxurious seafront bungalow. The other 'help' was a maid and cook. After prison, this place seemed like paradise. My duties were light and I spent many an hour just soaking up the sun. My employer was a gentle old soul with failing health. I decided not to rob him. As if in reward for my good deed, I formed a friendship with the cook and started fucking her. Life was very pleasant. Phylis Nye's cooking was delicious. After a while, pleasant becomes boring. I decided to move on, but this time with a partner. I thought a butler/cook combination might make job-seeking easier. I placed some well-worded advertisements in top people's magazines and *The Times*. The offers came rolling in. The old gent asked me to stay, offering me an increase in salary. I told him I would until he found a replacement. I remained another two weeks. At night, the old man's wife would ask me to take the jewels off her fingers. She liked me to put them in a glass of gin which she believed cleaned them.

I can't think of another time in my life when someone gave me their jewels ... and I gave them back. Once I left that house I never returned. These were two people I could not steal from.

Phylis and I moved into High Trees near Chalfont-St-Peters, Buckinghamshire. Our employer was a Mr Nigel Law, retired First Secretary of the Diplomatic Service.

Law lived in a mansion with his aristocratic Russian wife. Their life was opulent and incredibly gracious. Friends would fly in from Italy and America for lunch. After a meal and some relaxing drinks, they would fly back.

The Laws never dined alone; there were always guests. They were friends of the famous and I would hear all the latest gossip on Somerset Maugham's gay love triangle. The conversation was sparkling with wit, the house ablaze with shimmering silver and gold. It was like a palace. If I could have been born to their lifestyle, I would never have become a thief. As it was, I spent many happy hours examining Mrs Law's jewellery.

The Laws had a silver room, that is, a room where silver was stored. I had occasion to be looking in this room one day, when I found four boxes of soup spoons, they were so large that two spoonfuls would have emptied a bowl. I checked the inventory, they were not mentioned. I stored them away. A day or two later, I took a trip into the City. I packed all four boxes into a briefcase, and took the briefcase to the Silver Vaults. I told the man who dealt with me that I had inherited them. He weighed them and then paid me. I left £3,000 richer. A good working day.

Phylis worked away diligently. She was popular with other staff and employers and at night I pleased her. She knew nothing of my true nature.

Mrs Law kept her jewellery in the safe in their bedroom. It took me a while to figure out the maze that led to the object of my desires but, eventually, I did.

Mr Law wore a pocket watch, and on this watch chain were two keys. One of these keys opened a drawer in his dressing table, inside of which was another bunch of keys. One of these opened a tin box, the type that sailors had in olden days. Inside the tin box were two other keys. These opened the safe.

THE WICKED MR HALL

On one of my days off, I visited a friend of mine in Praed Street, Paddington, and I had the safe keys copied. Now that I had the keys, it was time to move on. I could not rob them while I was still working there. The first set of 'prints' that the police took would reveal me for who I was. I started answering adverts again.

My first interview was with a George Offat the Third. Offat was as ludicrously rich as the Laws. He had homes in Los Angeles and Virginia. The Virginia home was a mansion and ancestral seat. I was told that, if I took the position, I would have my own manservant, car and complete responsibility for a large household staff. I would have my own house on the estate and was assured that 'tips' would be so generous as to enable me not to touch my quite large salary. Apparently, the next door neighbour was a Mrs Dodge, widow of the motor magnate. This was the *crème de la crème* of American society, and I was to be the resident English butler. Offat flew to Greece, and from there sent an affidavit to the US government. He stated that I would not be a 'charge' to that country, that he would fly me back to the UK every year for a holiday, and would cover all medical bills.

Now I needed my green card. I picked up the relevant forms from the US embassy. At this stage, I said little to Phylis. As soon as I read through the forms I knew that, for me, there was no legal way of leaving the country. There was no way I could fit the criteria without having a completely fresh identity.

This was impossible – Offat already knew me as Roy Fontaine. If I completed these forms, there was a chance that I would be uncovered. Then I would lose what I already had. I couldn't risk it. The odds were too steep. I was glad I hadn't told Phylis. Even so, my feet were itchy and I wanted to move.

Sir George and Lady Aylwen liked Phylis and me. At my interview, as she read my forged references, I remember her saying that a reference wasn't worth the paper it was written on. She relied on her judgement. That was good! The next day she phoned High Trees, to check up on her prospective new butler. I answered the phone and, disguising my voice, gave a glowing testimonial to Roy Fontaine. Phylis and I were greeted with flowers and wine.

We now lived in Green Street, off Mayfair. Sir George was a former Lord Mayor of London and his Greek wife was many years younger than him. She controlled the household. In fact, she controlled everything, including her husband. Sir George went to bed early and alone.

The mistress was attracted to young foreign aristocrats. Wealth and titles don't always go hand in hand and I noted that some of her young lovers were actually rather 'down at heel'. I think this gave her the power and dominance in the relationships. Power and dominance, as I was soon to find out, were strong emotional drives in my new employer. There was something about her, an edge, a cruel edge. I would hear her in conversation with young men whom I knew shared her bed. She would pass remarks that were quite cutting. What made Lady Aylwen different from someone who just picked on another, was that she delighted in it. I felt it excited her to be cruel.

I had been there only a short while when she started to

play her games with me. One night I was summoned, time after time. I climbed the long staircase that led to her bedroom. The mistress was sitting up in bed, a low-cut negligée covering her breasts. She had dark blonde hair and resembled the late Marlene Dietrich. 'Bring me my cigarettes,' she demanded. I complied. After saying goodnight, I returned to my quarters downstairs. Only seconds passed before her bell rang again. 'I can't see my lighter. Find it for me.' Her gold cigarette lighter was inches away from her, in plain view. Again, I wished her goodnight and descended the staircase. Her bell was already ringing when I walked back into my room.

Once more I climbed the staircase. This time her instruction was beyond belief. The unlit cigarette was in her hand: 'Light me.' As a conscientious employee, I had never before been treated so contemptuously. Standing over her, I lit her cigarette. There was anger in my voice when I asked her whether she would require anything else of me before I retired for the evening. She remained silent for a few seconds, her eyes fixed on my crotch. I did feel excited. Having a beautiful sexy woman order you about and talk to you like you're a piece of shit can be an aphrodisiac. It wasn't an aphrodisiac I had been aware of until that precise second. Years before, I had thrashed a gay man with twigs until my arm ached. That had done nothing for me, but this was different. Without breaking her silence, she unzipped me. My cock was already semi-hard. She knew she had me. She told me to join her and I undressed and slid in beside her. The first touch of her manicured hand was soft. When we kissed, she squeezed my balls so hard I screamed. But I was still hard. I was learning something new about my sexuality. I expected her to go on top, but instead it was me who took the traditionally dominant position. When we started to have sex, I found out why. With each thrust, she slapped me. The blows were indiscriminate, landing on my thighs, my arse, my back. In between the slaps were scratches. Not the fingernails of a woman gripped by passion, these were scratches that lasted for seconds. She would dig her nails in with all her strength, and trawl them across my skin. While I was still inside her, her hands again found my testicles. She literally had me by the balls. All the time watching my face, she squeezed as I attempted to give her pleasure. I will never forget that cocktail of pain and pleasure. I was unable to separate what I was enjoying and what was just pure pain. I wondered whether she would want to piss on me or have me lick her arse. She didn't, but, if ordered, I would most probably have gone on my knees in compliance. Having all your power stripped from you, being controlled and humiliated while you orgasm, does strange things to you. It sheds light on dark corners of your psyche. The light that Lady Aylwen shone on me that night, I would have preferred to have left in shadow. I am not a man prone to introspection. Although she continued to taunt and excite me, I never again took up her offer. In the cold light of day, I like to be master of my own destiny. Until this day of writing, it has remained a repressed memory. It was two weeks before I could undress in front of Phylis.

I found the Aylwens a disappointment in many ways.

Although rich, their home was rather poorly furnished. The food they served was not of the best quality, nor was the wine. They either struggled to maintain their status or were just plain tight. They did, however, throw lavish parties. As guests arrived, the fur coats would be laid on a bed in one of the upstairs rooms. I would carry them up myself. Sometimes there would be jewels in the lapels, brooches. If I saw anything I fancied, I would take the brooch and place it underneath the bed. If someone called, the brooch could be found. If I didn't hear anything within forty-eight hours, I would sell it. It made trudging up and down the stairs worthwhile.

Not entirely happy in my work, I busied myself with the task of finding where the safe keys were. I searched high and low but there was no sign of them anywhere. In the end, my sights fell on Sir George's combination-locked briefcase. Patience is a virtue. Whenever I got the chance, I would play with the lock. I tried every combination of possible numbers – birthdays, anniversaries, ages, house numbers. Nothing. Eventually, one afternoon when Sir George was in the garden, I tried again. I stared at it and it hit me! One, two, three, four, and then O. O for open! On a day off, I took the keys to Praed Street and had copies made.

London life was not for Phylis. She was a country girl, raised in a village. Homely and eager to please, she wanted to go home. She asked me whether I would go with her, we could settle down, buy a shop, open a restaurant perhaps. Poor Phylis. I had never told her the truth about myself. We had grown close, I had bought her many gifts, taken her to Stafford to visit John and my mother. I told her to go back to her village and find an honest, homely man who would appreciate her. I did miss her for a while, but I was pleased I no longer had the responsibility. Sooner or later, I would cause her pain. I would always be a villain. I knew that. Phylis belonged in her village.

Charles Clore, on the other hand, could have bought a village. He was one of Britain's richest financiers, a powerful man. While at the Aylwens, his house had been pointed out to me. This was a man of immense wealth. I had a feeling about Clore. I wanted to work for him. I wanted to make him my biggest target, and rob him of millions.

I had these thoughts the very first time I heard of his name and of his wealth. When you are 'in service' you hear rumours. Upper-class circles are quite incestuous. The same people attend the same parties and there is a circuit of sorts. With Phylis gone, I had tired of the Aylwens. Also, the sooner I became just a memory, the sooner I could come back and rob the safe. I heard from one of the kitchen staff that Clore's butler had attempted suicide and was in hospital. Obviously, not a very happy individual. I was already scouring *Tatler* for a fresh appointment. When I saw the ad, although no details were given, I just knew that it was the Clore vacancy.

Clore was a small nervous man. He hated the dark and at night all lights had to be left on. At the time I knew him, he had recently divorced. He entertained ladies every evening, including Mandy Rice Davies, a young prostitute who became nationally famous and was later portrayed by Bridget Fonda in the film *Scandal*. When Bob Hope stayed in town, he was a house guest. Clore's wealth was greater than the Laws, or anybody else's that I'd worked for.

Original Renoir paintings hung on his walls. The place felt like someone had set up home in a museum. It was also like a fortress. Now that this man had untold wealth, the thought of losing it terrified him. Out of all the people I worked for, I found Clore the least personable. I wished I had robbed him destitute. Studying the contents, some of which I wanted to steal, was a most pleasurable pastime – jade cigarette boxes as big as bricks, a Fabergé Easter egg, worth half a million pounds, Picassos, gold statues. In his dining-room, every piece of furniture was antique. Clore and his designers would buy from the old, increasingly impoverished stately homes. The captains of industry are the new aristocracy. Clore's children would inherit more than some young Earl from a rambling country mansion. I eyed his belongings lasciviously, and tried to formulate a plan.

To tide myself over I went back and robbed the Laws' safe at High Trees. Some nice jewels. The cheapskate Aylwens also had their safe emptied. Clore was still proving to be a problem. I liked him less, and he had more. After robbing him, I wanted to go abroad. There was no reason why I couldn't make enough on this one job to last me the rest of my life. I could take millions in one hit. It would be complex, I would need the opportunity, instant buyers, and agreed prices. And a safe passage out of the country. But it was all here, the bloody Easter egg alone was worth half a million. I was working on the details when Clore had his insurance policy renewed.

Question. Are there any new employees in the house?

Answer. Yes, a butler.

Insurance investigators are very thorough. They found out who I was. Two of them, along with Clore's personal assistant who had originally engaged me, came to the house. I was told to pack my things and leave immediately. I made sure that one of them watched me pack. At this stage I had robbed nothing. I was sickened, I had been a whisker away from my biggest robbery. I consoled myself by spending a week at the Cumberland, one of London's nicer hotels. I drank brandies and had sex with young rent boys. At the end of the week I returned to the Knightsbridge area and rented a flat. However, while I had been putting my feet up at the Cumberland, the Old Bill had been busy. The front door to my new home suffered the same fate as the one in Hans Crescent. It was smashed in by sledgehammers wielded by officers of the Metropolitan Police. Once again it was 6.00am. Good job I'm not someone who likes to sleep late!

I was taken in and questioned about two jewel robberies, both of which I had done. I said nothing. I thought their evidence was at best circumstantial, but I never dreamed what would happen next. At the London County Sessions, they found me guilty. They gave me another ten years! As I walked down the dock steps, I swore that this time they could fuck themselves. I wasn't going to do this sort of time.

The sentences were ridiculous. I wouldn't do it! This time I'd earn that fucking 'E' patch they'd stuck on me for so many years. This time I would escape.

11
THREE'S A CROWD

Blundeston was ultra modern. Electronic. Escape proof. Well, we'd see about that. Like many of the modern prisons, it was built well away from the local community, a desolate place on a desolate part of the Suffolk coast. The wind off the North Sea would chill you to the bone.

I started doing my time quietly. There was plenty of scheming and planning going on there, but all escape attempts were uncovered. Somewhere, there was a grass. I told no one of my ideas, instead, I let it be known I was happy to do my time quietly. I'd been in worse prisons.

I was given a job in the kitchens. During the evening, while staring out of my cell window, I found myself staring at the roof of the place I worked. There were three mushroom-shaped ventilation shafts protruding from the flat surface. When you looked up in the kitchen, you looked at a flat ceiling, which meant that there must be another floor between the ceiling and the roof. I spoke to a con whom I thought to be trustworthy, George O'Neill.

George told me that the ventilator shafts came out of three rooms over the kitchen, two of which were used as stores, the third housed the boiler. Every week, a civilian worker came in to service them. Another con, Don Whittaker, was brought in. The three of us planned to escape.

Now that I knew what I was looking for, there was no problem, just work to do. When the civilian engineer came to do his service, I was waiting. As he sprayed around with his can of oil, I took an impression of his doorkey. I looked up at the circular shaft in the roof. There were no bars on it. While he had his head stuck between two pieces of machinery, reading some pressure dial or other, I stretched up and measured the width of the hole with a piece of string.

Later in my cell, I cut a hole in a sheet of newspaper to the exact circumference of the ventilation shaft. If I could get through the hole in that paper, I could get through the shaft. George O'Neill held it over my head. I could get through. We could all get out!

After doing some trade, I managed to get hold of a wrench. With George and Don acting as lookouts, I entered the boiler room. I carefully loosened all the bolts to the mushroom-shaped canopies. Now the canopies could be unscrewed by hand and lifted off. A man could clamber up the small shaft and pull himself up on to the roof.

We were almost ready. I made a phone call to a friend in London. He would bring a getaway car with the key taped under the dashboard. If we made it out of the prison, we would have to somehow get out of this desolate shithole before the roadblocks were set up. We had the sea on one side of us, and bleak countryside stretching as far as the eye could see, to the other.

Prisons are full of routines. I had come to know the routine of the kitchen. Every night, just before it closed, the kitchen officer would hand a selected prisoner a list. This was then taken down to the principal warder's office. The list would contain the names of three men. It was the duty of these men to get the tea urns started, the porridge on, and generally bringing the kitchen to life. Their cell doors were unlocked an hour before everyone else's. When they started work, the prison was virtually still asleep. We needed our names on that list. Don stole a sheet of the same type of paper that the list was written on.

The date was now due for the car to be delivered. We had to make our move. Each day increased our chances of being discovered as a random cell search could reveal the duplicate key.

That evening, as the kitchen closed, I watched the kitchen officer hand the usual con the list for the early-morning shift. Taking it, he meandered through the kitchen. He stopped to chat to another prisoner. I approached him. He was holding the list almost absentmindedly as he talked. I pointed to it, I don't know if I sounded casual, but I was trying: 'Principal Warder's office?'

He nodded. 'I'm just going down that way myself, I'll drop it in for you, if you want.'

He handed me the list, my heart was beating like crazy.

We had it! I walked out of the kitchen at what I hoped was a usual pace. Once in the corridor I hurried to my cell. I copied the list, exactly. All except for the names, of course.

The next morning Fontaine, O'Neill and Whittaker would be unlocked early. I hurried down to the Principal's office, there was no one there. I put the list on his desk. I got word to the other two. None of us slept that night. I spent the hours between darkness and light, staring out of the window. I could taste the freedom. I had stolen some pepper from the stores and I'd told the other two to do the same.

If all went well, we would be free in a few hours. If that happened they would get the dogs out as soon as our escape was known. They would bring the dogs to our cells and our blankets and sheets would be put under the hounds' noses to give them our scent. I sprinkled black pepper over everything, including myself. Apart from a sneezing fit, the dogs would get nothing. I sat and waited.

It was still dark, and I was still staring out the window when the kitchen lights went on. It was 5.30am. I watched the warder come out of the kitchen building and enter our wing. I listened to his footsteps in the corridor. Without bothering to look in, he unlocked my door. Within minutes all three of us were in the kitchen. Locking the door behind us, we entered the boiler room. Unscrewing the bolts to the mushroom canopy, I crawled up and on to the roof. The other two followed. Carefully we replaced it.

Our escape route was not obvious to follow. Silently, and still under cover of darkness, we crept along the roof and from there, on to the prison church. Over that one, down a drainpipe, into a yard. Keeping close to the walls and praying for the darkness not to lift too quickly, we made our way to a maintenance yard where we knew there were ladders. Taking one long and one shorter ladder we crept up to the perimeter barbed-wire fence. We extended the ladder and, first taking the small ladder up, tossed it as quietly as we could over to the other side. Standing precariously, one foot on the top rung of the ladder, the other on the springy, vicious roll of barbed wire that lay on top of the fence, we each jumped. Whittaker cut his leg quite badly. Picking up the smaller ladder, we scaled the final wall that stood between us and freedom.

The scream of the sirens cut through the early morning air like a knife. Whittaker's leg was now bleeding badly. He knew he was slowing us down. He told us to leave him. O'Neill and I grabbed an arm each and, putting it over our shoulders, ran with him. We made our way through bushes and over some fields. Before we were across the fields, we heard the barking. They had the dogs on us. We ran on to where the car was waiting.

The man I had phoned about the car was a supposed old friend who was indebted to me for many favours. He ceased to be a friend that day. There was no car. We were three escaped prisoners in uninhabited, bleak countryside. The wind coming off the North Sea was harsh and chilling, one of us was injured. What a friend. What a cunt.

Our original plan had been to get across the bridge at Lowestoft before the roadblocks went up. I knew that there was no chance. As the barking of the dogs drew nearer, we half-crouched and half-ran through the wet, cold fields. We took cover wherever we could.

An RAF helicopter from nearby Lowestoft took to the skies in search of us. We crouched under bushes when we heard its approaching noise. Sometimes the dogs got quite close. We kept moving. All that day Don Whittaker, George O'Neill and myself ran through field after field, our hands and necks scratched by the undergrowth that acted as our cover. The blood around Don's wound had now congealed, but his leg was in a sorry state. He was slowing us down.

As each hour passed, I became hungrier, colder and more resolute. I would rather die than be put back in prison. There were times during the coming night when I wondered if I would. By the time darkness fell, we were all disorientated. It was impossible to tell how far we'd travelled. From the fields we could see the lights of the police roadblocks. We travelled until exhaustion overcame us. We slept huddled under a hedge, our bodies frozen.

There were still a couple of hours of darkness left when I awoke the other two. We moved on. We had reached a village of some kind where there was a river to cross. As people slept, we crept through their back gardens, sticking to the riverbank. We needed to get across. I wanted to swim, neither George nor Don could. We retraced our steps and started checking the garden sheds. We were all convinced that if we could get across the river we would be past the roadblocks. There could be an inflatable dinghy in one of the sheds.

On about the fourth garden, we opened a shed and

found an Indian-style canoe for three people. There were no paddles, so we took garden spades. Lowering the canoe into the water, we set off. The current began to pull us downstream. The river carried us along easily, each foot taking us further and further from the prison. My feet and body ached, I was happy to let the flow of the water replace my weary footsteps.

In the dark we were carried on our way. As daybreak came, we passed two all-night fishermen on the bank. They looked at us as we approached then, raising their flasks, shouted: 'Good luck, lads'. They wouldn't inform. A sporting chance from sportsmen. Before the dark had fully lifted, we berthed on the opposite bank. We let the canoe carry on its journey downstream.

We walked for about a mile. It was now light. There was an unattended van about ten feet away from the roadside house where, presumably, its owner lived. Releasing the handbrake, we pushed it twenty or thirty feet down the lane. When we felt that the noise of the engine wouldn't disturb the household, we hot wired it. For the first time since the breakout, we had a vehicle. It was good to be moving at something quicker than a snail's pace and it was good to be warm. We were about half-a-mile outside the village of Beccles, when the van ran out of petrol. Soon people would be up and about. We were bedraggled and dirty. We needed the cover of a vehicle, and we had to get out of this area.

We walked quickly to the edge of the village. Don was hobbling badly. If anyone saw him, suspicion would be aroused. We stole the first car we saw. We drove through the village looking for signposts. We turned a corner into a house-lined street, heading west. We all froze as, in the distance, we saw a lone police car. An officer with a torch was standing next to it. George was driving. I hissed at him: 'Carefully, drive into the next driveway and walk straight to the garage doors.'

George did as I said. The noise of the gravel under the wheels sounded like exploding bombs. We turned the engine off. Our eyes were continually on the house. Would the lights go on? Had we woken them? George walked to the garage door and opened it. I peered through the hedge for any sign of movement from the police car. I listened for the crackle of his radio, but heard nothing. George crept back to the car. I heard voices, a woman.

Silently, I got out of the car, crept to the hedge and looked through. The front door was open and a woman, dressed for work, was talking to the policeman. She seemed agitated and the patrolman followed her into her house. Firing the engine, we drove out of the driveway and back in the direction that we'd come. We took the first secondary road we could. Within minutes we were clear of the village.

I stopped at a newsagents and bought cigarettes, chocolate and newspapers. We devoured the chocolate, and read reports of our escape in the papers. I was the only one of us with money. We had seven pounds. Not enough to take us to Scotland, but I had some friends to the west of where we were. We filled the tank. Coasting on the adrenalin surge that only the chased know, we drove inland. All of us were desperate for sleep.

THREE'S A CROWD

An hour-and-a-half later, I pulled the car to the side of the road. I had chosen this particular friend because he had no criminal record. There was no reason why the authorities would connect him with me. Even so, I looked about. Everything seemed normal, a suburban house in a suburban street. Blundeston was now a long way away. I told the other two to stay put. Getting out of the car, I approached the house. I went straight round to the back door, knocking lightly, I entered.

At the kitchen sink, washing dishes, was my friend's wife. She looked at me with mild surprise: 'You've been on the television.'

I nodded, all the time trying to sense her mood. Would she help? 'I have two colleagues down the road in a car, can I bring them in?'

Wiping her hands, she nodded. Her husband was an old acquaintance of mine, he was not a criminal, but had benefited from my crime. They were both brilliant. They did all they could for us. We bathed Don's leg and then bandaged it. We all bathed and shaved. The husband went to his wardrobe and gave us whatever fitted us. Jackets, jumpers, trousers – none of us had a complete change of clothes, but we all had something. We might have looked motley, but not like escaped cons any more. They had £80 in the house, which they gave me. After feeding us, they wished us luck. I would repay them. I never forget that kind of loyalty.

With full stomachs, clean clothes and looking like ordinary human beings, we hit the road again. I had many contacts in Glasgow and we started the drive to Scotland.

Don's leg still prevented him from driving, so George and I took it in turns.

We travelled throughout the night. With sleep, our instincts and spirits were returning to normal. We had beaten them. We had beaten their walls and bars and their roadblocks. My only concern now was the car. It had been ten hours since the theft, they would almost certainly have connected it to us. By now, the make and registration number would have been communicated to every police force in Britain.

Again, the black blanket of the night seemed like a friend. As daybreak approached, the Glasgow skyline broke through the morning mist. I drove off the main road and started to follow the winding route of the Clyde. At a quiet spot, Dalmuir, we turned the engine off and rolled down all the windows. The three of us pushed the car over the bank and into the dirty grey water of the Clyde. The river swallowed the car in seconds. The last trace with Norfolk was now gone.

The police could guess where we would go, but they had no leads to follow. The trail was as cold as the water covering the getaway car. After a short walk, we caught a bus into the city. From there I made a phonecall. A jailbreak in Norfolk is no big deal in Glasgow. The friend I'd called knew nothing of Blundeston. In careful language, I told him the situation.

He picked us up in a central carpark. We then drove to his home, where he sent his wife out to buy us all new clothes. Before we put them on, we slept for fifteen or sixteen hours. The next day, my new host pressed £250 into my hand. I made another phonecall. An old contact came round with a bent driving licence.

That afternoon I hired a car. Since the escape, we had relied on the goodwill of friends. Now it was time for us to resume work and pay our own way. It obviously wasn't a good idea for the three of us to remain together, but to separate we needed capital. I was given some information and we went to work.

There was a jeweller who lived on the outskirts of Perth, a wealthy man, with a nice, large detached house. For unknown reasons, probably tax evasion, this man was thought to keep large amounts of jewellery and cash in his home. I was assured that the job was simplicity itself and that the information was good. The three of us drove to the man's house. The owner would be at work. It was easy getting in and we searched all the downstairs rooms.

We worked from bottom to top, searching methodically as we went. So far nothing. On the top floor, a bedroom door was locked. George O'Neill, a strong man, put his boot to the lock, and the door flew open. Lying there on the bed was a woman in late middle age. The first thing that I saw, besides her face, was the phone on the bedside table. She caught my gaze: 'I've already phoned the police.' She was very cool and, my instincts thought, truthful! As I went down the stairs, I thought, fuck! If we didn't have shitty luck, we wouldn't have any luck at all.

As I descended the last few stairs into the hallway. I saw the hazy outline of two police motorcyclists through the frosted glass of the front door. One was already approaching. He rang the bell. I took a deep breath and through the closed door, I asked him what he wanted. He said there had been a 999 call, reporting a burglary. I laughed, and said: 'Oh that, that was just a silly mistake. That stupid cat breaking things again.' He asked me to open the door.

'Certainly, certainly, just let me put a bathrobe on, I've just got out of the shower.' Once out of his line of vision, I raced for the back door. George and Don were already through it and running. As I followed, one of the patrolmen appeared round the corner. He saw my face. I ran. Miraculously Don Whittaker, even with his still injured leg, managed to get away. George O'Neill had taken off up a hill. I followed. So did the two policemen. George and I had been chased along coastland by dogs, we had huddled in frozen fields, starved. We knew what capture meant. Policemen don't know punishment blocks. There was a desperation to our running that they could not match. Turning back, they talked into their radios instead. The terrain was very moorish, we crossed the brink of the hill and were out of sight.

We came upon what looked like quite an expensive hotel. Brown wooden ranch fencing surrounded the car park. Even to a hunted man, it looked picturesque. We looked around the grounds. I debated stealing a car, but then we spotted a large, luxury bungalow that stood apart from the main hotel. Casually, we strolled up to the front door and knocked. There was no answer. Within seconds we were in. We quickly searched the place and found clothes that fit. We both changed. The police description of us no longer fitted.

THREE'S A CROWD

Looking out of the window, I noticed a bus pull into the carpark. I checked my watch. It was the top of the hour. If that bus was hourly, we could be on the next one. George found a jewel case under a pile of nylon stockings. I looked at the pieces. There was a few thousand pounds there. Staying in the bungalow was dangerous, so I suggested to George that we hide in the grounds. When the next bus came we would board, separately. As we left the bungalow, both now wearing smart, dark overcoats, I picked up a locked briefcase, purely for image. As I had hoped, two minutes past the top of the hour, a bus pulled into the drive. George and I approached the bus from different angles. We boarded separately, both buying return tickets. Old people and children can sometimes make good cover. I took the opportunity to talk to an elderly lady. It almost looked like we were together.

As the bus made its way down the winding lanes that would eventually take it to Perth, we turned a corner to see two police cars blocking the road. My enthusiasm for chatting to the old lady intensified – the less eye contact I had with the police, the better. One officer got on board and questioned the driver. Another walked slowly round the vehicle, staring at the passengers. I gave him a glance and then talked to the old lady like my life depended on it. The bus was waved on. Our, for once not shitty, luck was holding. Back in Glasgow the three of us were reunited. I sold the jewels. The Perth police had 'made' me. The car we left outside the jeweller's house had been rented in Glasgow. The Glasgow police knew me and would be looking for me. Another bent licence, another hired car. We moved on to Edinburgh and another safe house.

We split the jewel money three ways and went on a shopping spree for new clothes, and had some nights out. It was good to be back in the real world. It had been an exciting week. The briefcase that I had stolen from the bungalow had been opened. It belonged to Jeremy Hindley, the racehorse trainer. It contained his 'Stud Book'.

The police were looking for us, the question was how seriously? We drove south. Not to London, as was usual, but this time to Dover. From there, we sent postcards to Blundeston. Let them think we had crossed the water into mainland Europe. George and Don wanted to destroy Hindley's 'Stud Book', it was just one more connection to one more crime. I said: 'No, this is a record of all his horses' pedigrees. It goes back years, he might not have another copy. Let's be sportsmen, let's send it back.' We wrote a postcard, printing a letter each, explaining who we were. We sent it to his home in Clitheroe, Lancashire. At this point, I thought George and Don would want to go their separate ways, but they seemed happy for us to continue working as a team. Personally, I thought that once the prison had the postcards Interpol would keep a vague eye out for us. For the overworked police here, we would be just another file that would go to the bottom of the pile. Turning the car round, we returned to Glasgow.

12

A CLOSE SHAVE

When you are a known villain, ordinary people love to give you information. It's as if they break the law by proxy. Associating with criminals seems to hold a fascination for some. They wouldn't want to do the crime, or the time, but they like to buy you drinks, possibly because then they think you're on their side. Perhaps it makes them feel safe.

One evening, while out drinking, a Glaswegian bookmaker whispered into my ear. He told me of another bookie, with whom he shared the same accountant. The accountant had inadvertently mentioned that this bookmaker had asked his advice about how to avoid paying tax on a sizeable sum of money. The accountant had said the easiest way was not to bank it or declare it, but if your house was secure, to keep it at home.

Although there were differences, this sounded like a re-run of Perth. I was very wary, but I would consider it. Together with Don and George, I drove around Glasgow looking at this man's shops. They were all shabby, corner street establishments. All in poor working-class districts. I felt doubtful about the information. Surely these shops couldn't turn over that kind of money? We found out the man's address and drove out to look at his house. This was very different, a large bungalow standing in its own grounds. Double garage. Quite an expensive property.

After Perth, I was in no rush to break in and start searching only to be running from the Old Bill ten minutes later. This time, we sat and watched the house for two days. It looked like a small, middle-aged woman and a short, middle-aged man, the bookie, lived there. It seemed they lived alone. We decided to go in posing as the police. We'd see whether we could make him think we were just confiscating the money.

The next morning, all of us suitably dressed, we knocked loudly on his door. His wife answered. As she half-opened the door, I pushed past telling her we were police. Looking up the stairs I saw her husband come out of their bedroom, pulling on a dressing-gown. He called down the stairs: 'What is it?'

I answered him: 'We're the police, sir, we have reason to believe there is an amount of stolen currency in the house. I have a warrant and I propose to search your home.'

He walked down the stairs. He didn't seem surprised. Placing my briefcase on a coffee table, I looked around the room. I was growing into my role as a supposed Detective Inspector. I told George and Don to start searching the upstairs rooms. At this point his wife spoke: 'Have you asked to see their warrant?'

George and Don stopped their ascent of the stairs in mid-stride. The shocked bookmaker realised his mistake: 'Can I see your search warrant, Inspector?'

'Certainly, sir.' I opened the briefcase and pretended to look for it. George and Don were now back in the room, each of them close to the middle-aged owners. Looking up from the case, I spoke in an assuringly calm voice: 'I'm afraid it will be impossible for you to see the warrant, sir, because I'm afraid you're being robbed. Sorry!'

The couple looked around. They knew they were in our power. As the leader, the bookmaker threatened me: 'You'll never get away with this. I know every villain in Glasgow.'

I just smiled: 'But you don't know me, do you? And right at this moment, I'm the only one that counts.' We tied them both up. My two accomplices started the search.

Every so often they came back to me with small wads of money – £1,000, £1,500 – but nothing near £50,000. Some jewellery boxes were found, from Edwards in Buchanan Street. I had done their window years before with Johnny Collins. I also knew that it had been robbed just a few weeks ago. I looked at the jewellery; it was not the type his wife would wear. The bookie was a 'fence'. Although it hadn't fulfilled its promise, it wasn't too bad a day's work. We'd each earned a few thousand. A few miles down the road we phoned the police and gave them the bookmaker's address. We told them they should investigate.

THE WICKED MR HALL

For the police, this would have been just another bungled robbery attempt. I didn't think the bookmaker would be keen to give evidence about what was taken. Back at my friend's house we had a few drinks and relaxed.

A young woman arrived and we were introduced as three friends from London. She probably guessed our occupation. We were all invited by her to a party that night. My friend's wife took me to one side and warned me off. The house where the party was to be held was known by police. There would be a chance of a raid. Don and I took notice. George, who fancied the girl who had invited us, insisted that he went. I said: 'OK, but don't take too much money with you, you might end up getting searched.'

That night, George was arrested. We got the information in the early hours of the morning. Don and I got dressed, thanked our hosts, who promised to keep us informed of what happened, and left. George O'Neill's freedom had come to an abrupt end. I wondered whether he would be returned to Blundeston, and if he did, would he end up looking at the postcards he had helped send.

In London, I booked into the Dorchester, Don into the Cumberland. After a couple of days' rest we moved on, this time to Cornwall. Being fugitives, we had no base. If you have no home you can go to, the natural inclination is to keep moving. We did a few tourist things, visited a couple of castles, went to Land's End. Although we had earned a few grand during the short period since our escape, we were spending freely. I spotted a jewellers in Falmouth. Don Whittaker had never done a smash and grab before, so I took him through the routine.

A CLOSE SHAVE

We 'hit' this seaside jewellers in broad daylight. Don smashed, I grabbed. We were less than fifty feet away from the shop when a police car, sirens blazing, gave chase. I am not a great driver, but by driving with life-threatening abandon, I eventually managed to lose them. We decided to separate. I gave Don some funds and told him I'd meet him in London. I drove back to the hotel to pick up the few things we both had. As I entered the hallway, I heard two women guests saying, 'Criminals! Staying here, imagine it!'

I wondered whether I had enough time to pick up our suitcases. I walked upstairs to the corridor where my room was, the door was ajar. I turned around and headed back for the staircase. I hadn't actually started to descend when I saw the two detectives standing in the foyer. Through a window, I could see uniformed officers in the garden at the back of the hotel. There was no way out. I climbed the stairs as far as they would take me and I knocked on the first door I came to. No answer. I tried the handle and the door opened. The room was quite small. There was a woman's personal belongings on the dresser. The only hiding place was under the bed, so that is where I went. I lay flat on the floor, my cheek against the carpet. I regulated my breathing until it was barely audible. If I could, I would wait for nightfall. I lay still, and dreaded the thought of returning to prison. I must have been there for two or three hours before I heard voices. Two girls were on the other side of the door. One said: 'Well, I'm not sleeping in there tonight, not until I'm sure they're not here.' The door opened and I heard two sets of footsteps. My ears were the only sensory organ that was of any use to me. Each sound was intensified. I heard the wardrobe door being opened, the curtains being drawn, and then the counterpane, inches from my eyes, was lifted. I expected screams, but the noise still shocked me. I hadn't seen her face, so she must have seen my arm or hand. The screams became words as the young women ran screaming out of the room. 'They're here! They're here!' I pulled myself out from under the bed and, with my body stiff from immobility, tried to shake it into life and ran for the door. The screams of 'They're here' were distant now, downstairs. I remember feeling annoyed as I ran – what did they mean 'They! They!' I was on my fucking own! From a first floor window, I jumped into a soft, earthy, flowerbed. I ran through the back of the gardens, over a fence and on into the night. I never saw any police.

I ended up on what must have been one of the roads out of Falmouth. I walked for hours, eventually coming upon a small village. There was a sign 'Car for Hire', so I knocked on the door. I told the man who answered that I had been in a road accident, another car had forced me off the road, my wife had been taken to Exeter Hospital, and I desperately needed to reach her. After agreeing a price, he agreed to drive me. I covered my muddy shoes and lower trousers with a travelling rug. It was just as well. A few miles down the road, a police unit stopped us. The officer seemed to know the driver. He gave me a cursory glance. As he did I lit a cigar. The driver was told to be on the lookout for two men, on foot, who were wanted for a jewel robbery. We drove on. We were stopped a second time, same thing. After that, I slept.

A CLOSE SHAVE

It was the middle of the night when the driver woke me. We were in the car park of Exeter Hospital. I paid him and thanked him. Then, with him still watching, I walked into the hospital. I went to a window, where I could observe him leaving. Once he'd left, so did I. I booked myself into a hotel, cleaned myself up so that I no longer resembled a man who'd spent half the night running through people's back gardens and, in the morning, caught the first train to London. After phoning Don Whittaker to make sure he'd also made it back, I met my buyer and sold the proceeds from the Falmouth jewel raid. The fate of George O'Neill had been on both our minds. The three of us had been through a lot together. There was nothing in the papers. If we could help George, we certainly couldn't do it from here. Although it could be risky, we decided we would try. If nothing else, we could get a third, unknown party to visit him, smuggle him money, dope, whatever would make his life a little easier. Again, we went north. If we had known what this journey held in store we would never have walked to the car.

Somebody once said: 'The best laid plans of mice and men ...' You can plan and arrange all you want, but when random chance enters your life, it can all come to naught. The news on George O'Neill was as bad as it could be. They knew who he was, but before he could be returned to an English prison he would be prosecuted for offences that occurred in Scotland. He was to be put in a 'line up' on suspicion of involvement in the Perth jeweller's break-in and the Glasgow bookmaker's robbery. Don and I went out to buy him what we could. A non-criminal friend had

131

agreed to act as visitor. It is an inbuilt instinct of mine never to attract the attention of police. Unless I am fleeing from a crime, I never speed. I don't jump lights or shout my mouth off. The police take an active enough interest in my life without me stupidly bringing myself to their attention. Driving carefully was now an ingrained habit with me and, this day travelling through Glasgow, was no exception. The first inkling that this day would be worse than the average was the sound and feel of crushed metal and shattering glass. Don and I were thrown forward as a Volkswagen Beetle full of drunken students ploughed into the back of us. The German car flipped, landing on its roof. What had been a fairly deserted street, was suddenly full of spectators.

A crowd started to gather around us. We both knew that, if we waited for the police to arrive, we might just as well give ourselves up. Various vehicles stopped to see whether they could help. Some of the students were quite badly injured. When a taxi pulled up, Don grabbed the driver and said: 'My friend has injured his chest, I need to get him to the hospital. Will you take us?' The cab driver nodded and we both got in. I lay back and feigned injury. In truth we were physically fine. Emotionally, we were in a panic. We had to get away from the scene as quickly as possible. I could see the hospital gates. Once through them, we'd walk into Casualty and out through some other exit, carless, pissed off, but still at liberty. The taxi driver had his indicator on, ready to turn, when the last thing in the world we wanted to happen, happened. A police patrol car cut in front of us. Two policemen approached the car. My moans grew in intensity and frequency. I closed my eyes and acted my heart out. Don responded to the policeman's questions: 'Excuse me, sir, but were you involved in a car accident a few minutes ago?'

Don replied: 'They just drove straight into the back of us! My friend has a chest injury. I must get him to the hospital.' As if to confirm this I moaned loudly and dramatically.

The policeman continued: 'Don't you realise, that it is a crime to leave the scene of an accident?'

Don's acting was easily as good as mine: 'My friend! My friend is badly hurt, he's crushed his chest. All I thought of was hospital!' Whether they believed us or not didn't matter, procedure is procedure. The police needed statements, they needed identities, proof of ownership. They needed to fill in their report sheets. Don was asked to get out of the taxi and accompany one of the officers to the station. The other would stay with me. Although the police officers didn't know it and, although Don would not voluntarily tell them, he knew, as I did, that his liberty was at an end.

After all we had been through, climbing through the air vents at Blundeston, Don tearing his leg apart on the barbed wire fence, chased by dogs through fields, chased by the police in Falmouth, chased by the police in Perth, each time outrunning them, only for half-a-dozen pissed students, totally unaware of the consequences of their actions, to have us captured.

After initial tests at the hospital, they took me for an X-ray. I lay on the trolley waiting for the procedure to begin.

The doctor left the room, saying he would just be a minute. Outside in the corridor, the officer assigned to watch me paced up and down, looking through the glass-windowed door every few seconds. Parallel to me, less than a foot away, was an unlocked sash window. It was open just a few inches. As the officer's head vanished from view, I put my hand under the window and raised it a few inches, it moved easily. For this I was grateful. If he noticed any change in the window, he would be in the room immediately. If the doctor returned, my chance was gone. I pushed the window up again. Now there was enough room for me to roll through and out into the gardens. I could see the tops of flowers if I lifted my head slightly. The officer's head appeared at the glass, once more he looked at me. As his head vanished, I pulled the trolley into the window and rolled. As my body felt the hard sand and cement windowsill, my movement stopped. The flowerheads that I could see were on an embankment. I was on the first floor, not the ground. I heard the door open, peripheral vision revealed a blue police uniform. I rolled. The drop must have been fifteen feet and I landed badly, one leg under the other, my body hitting the ground flat. The only thing greater than the pain was the fear of capture. Somehow, I stood and ran. There were shouts and screams behind me. I was becoming used to that. Being chased was happening with alarming regularity. I was becoming a bit of an athlete. I got out of the hospital grounds and, after running blindly, found myself at the bottom of a block of tenement flats.

There were two huge industrial-sized dustbins, behind

which were cardboard boxes and other misplaced rubbish. I squeezed in between the bins, and got behind them. I moved into the rubbish. Nestling myself in like some bug, I covered myself with other people's shite. I was cold and shaken, and my nerves were on edge. But I would not be taken. I would sit in my own piss before I'd let that happen. Darkness was still four or five hours away. Until then, I would sit here. When the piss came, I just let it go. It ran where it ran. I was hurt, cold and rancid. But I was still free. I knew that if the great God Almighty were to appear in either George O'Neill's or Don Whittaker's prison cells, and ask them whether they'd like to be free, as long as they sat under rubbish with piss soaking into their crotches for a few hours, they'd have jumped at the chance. Sometimes it is good to think and be grateful for small mercies.

I sat hunched in one position, way past the falling of dusk. My joints ached and screamed for freedom of movement. My mouth was bone dry from lack of liquid and fresh oxygen. Sometimes, I think of the supposedly austere life of those Zen monks in Tibet, the ones who endure hours of stillness for spiritual enlightenment. Well, there are times when their lifestyle is no harder than that of your average Scottish villain. I must say, that as I crawled out from under the tenement garbage, I didn't feel particularly spiritual. Fucked off is, I think, the correct term.

I enjoyed the walk to the phone box, almost as much as some Turkish baths I've had. To stretch my cramped muscles was almost heaven. I phoned a friend, then stepped back into the darkness and waited. A short while later a car drew alongside the phone booth. A young man who I'd never seen before got out. He seemed to be looking for someone and he paced up and down. After what I had been through, I was feeling extremely cautious. The young man obviously had no wish to use the phone. If he was waiting for someone to call him, he wouldn't keep wandering so far from the box. I wasn't entirely sure but, if he had come for me, I didn't want him to drive off. I stepped out from the shadows and crossed the road. He looked at me. Although he didn't know me, there seemed to be some relief at my appearing. He spoke first: 'Are you Roy?' The words were like a fine brandy being poured down my throat. We got in the car and drove away. I read in the papers the next day about two escaped convicts who had been involved in a car accident in the city centre. One was in custody, the other had made a daring escape. I was glad they didn't have any details. It wasn't that glamorous.

Both my friends had been caught. The threesome was at an end. It was time for me to go my own way. Time for me to leave Scotland.

13

ALMOST A
FAMILY MAN

In London I remembered that Turkish baths were preferable to walking, stiff joints or no stiff joints. Besides the baths, I ate in nice restaurants and stayed in a decent hotel. I deserved a rest. Margaret was a lovely young girl. She was Irish, from Dublin, and twenty years my junior. I met her at the Connaught. In my life, I have been a bastard. I have killed for money or self-preservation, but there is a bit of good in the worst of us, and a bit of bad in the best.

With Margaret, I gave my best. She was a sweet, lost soul who appealed to my better instincts. I loved her, but was never 'in love' with her. She sat alone in the bar, nursing a martini. I have known loneliness, and that is what I sensed in her. I asked the waiter to invite her over for a drink and she accepted. We got on immediately. The next day we arranged to meet.

Her father was a headmaster, her brother a sergeant in the Irish police. This was her first time away from home and it seemed as though she had had a strict, claustrophobic upbringing. She had come to London to start a new life and had some savings, but not much. I suggested that we book into another hotel, this time with her as my guest.

That night we went to bed. It was a few days later when she told me that she was two months pregnant. She had run from shame. I have never lived by society's rules and when I see rules and misguided beliefs that force a young girl to run from her home and community for the sin of making love, I'm glad that I don't. When she asked me what I did for a living, I told her that I was a businessman. It was nice to have female company. I dared not think too far into the future, but if I was still around when the baby was born, I would look after it. We rented a flat off Regent Street. I was almost a family man.

When Margaret asked questions about what I was doing, where I was going, I would just say 'business'. She would kiss me goodbye, satisfied with the explanation. I got in contact with some old friends and we robbed Gerrards, the Regent Street jewellers.

Thieves need inside information, inside help. Plenty of people have criminal tendencies if not criminal aptitude. With these people, if you pay them, you'll get them. Cash is a great lure. If they thought for any length of time about what they were doing, they would back out in fear of court or prison. But if you say, here's so much, just do this one thing, no one will ever know, the chances are, they'll do it.

ALMOST A FAMILY MAN

Two such people came to my attention in that autumn of 1964. Both were corruptible and both were employed in pertinent jobs. I'll call them 'X' and 'Y'. I won't name them, for their families' sakes. These people were civilians, not villains.

On a Sunday evening, with the city almost deserted, myself and two colleagues drew up outside Gerrards. It was exactly two minutes to seven. At seven o'clock, we stepped out of the car and, using keys supplied by Y, removed the padlocks, putting dummy ones in their place. A half a mile away X, who worked in the burglar alarm office that covered Regent Street, switched off the alarms. We entered.

Three minutes later the burglar alarms in Regent Street were again fully functional. For two hours, we rifled through and took the most valuable gems in stock. Back in the burglar alarm office, at one minute to nine, the alarms were switched off again.

At 9.00pm exactly, the three of us coolly walked out of a much poorer Gerrards. Two minutes later, the street was again under the protection of electronic alarm systems. We had stolen hundreds of thousands of pounds worth of jewels. As I would cryptically tell Margaret, it was business! There were only a few thieves who would fit the profile for this job. I knew that I was one. The hunt for me would be stepped up. I thought it would be a good idea to leave London.

In the Cavendish Hotel, Eastbourne, I read about the Gerrards robbery. Among the items we had stolen had been a tiara, necklace, bracelet and ring, all set with diamonds and emeralds, all belonging to the Broadway star Beatrice Lilley. Lilley's losses were quite high that night. She wasn't the only woman to lose a piece that was probably irreplaceable – the Marchioness of Abergavenny lost a tiara that was literally ablaze with diamonds. Putting to one side any thoughts about the sadness and loss of those I had robbed, I went out on the town with Margaret.

Margaret was well suited to me in that she loved the high life. We both adored the thrill of casino gambling, eating the best food and living life with a zest. Sex was good, her body was young and firm. She was passive and enthusiastic at the same time. I was her guide, her Svengali. The pregnancy at this stage was still not showing.

I was a forty-year-old thief on the run, pulling off good jobs, making a fortune and sleeping with a woman half my age who was in love with me. Life was picking up. To compare washing up in a prison kitchen with this just couldn't be done.

As good as hotels are, after a while you start to tire of them and you want the privacy that only your own home can bring. I started checking the property columns in the papers. I found a farmhouse in Paddock Wood, Kent. Now we had a home with three bedrooms, large lounge, country kitchen, conservatory and fields all around us.

The owner of the farm was a lady called Mrs Nielsen. I introduced myself as Roy Philips, the same surname I had given Margaret on our first meeting. I had taken the trouble in London to dispose of all documentation that would identify me as Roy Fontaine. I told my new landlady that Margaret and I had been recently married. Nielsen herself lived in a static caravan at the end of the garden. Close to retirement age, I felt sorry for her. Having to rent out your own home while you live in a caravan, just to make ends meet, must be hard. I would often invite her into the house for drinks. She became close to Margaret and myself, and friendship and trust soon followed.

Life at Paddock Wood soon settled into a very agreeable routine. The farm was peaceful and private. We joined the local country club, gambled at weekends and were accepted by the local community as a successful mature businessman and his young wife.

Being nosey can sometimes have its compensations. Our landlady intrigued me – there was something I wasn't quite sure of. It could be that I can smell money. One evening, when we sat down to drinks in front of the fire, I told Margaret to keep Mrs Nielsen in conversation while I looked in her caravan. While our ageing host drank my whisky, I looked through her drawers. I found her bank statements. Not only wasn't she poor, she was very comfortably off. My sympathy evaporated like hot air.

In the 1960s, there was a long-running American TV show called *The Fugitive.* This was very popular in the UK and was one of the programmes that Margaret and I took to watching. At some point during every episode, Margaret would comment: 'Oh, I do hope he gets away.' Now I can lie with the best of them, but when you live with someone, when you become close to someone, the truth gnaws at you. Secrets can become like burdens and, the closer we became, the heavier my load seemed to be. I longed to tell her. Not least, so that she could be prepared if I was ever captured. As the credits rolled, I turned towards her: 'What would you say if I told you that I was like him!' I nodded towards the screen. She just laughed, not even bothering to look at me.

Then it just came out. I was aware that all humour had left my voice. 'I am like him. I'm a fugitive, an escaped prisoner.' Margaret now turned her head to look at me, her eyes searched mine for a sign that I was joking. There was none.

'You're serious?' she asked.

I nodded: 'I'm a thief. Always have been. As you may imagine, I'm very good at it.'

She laughed again. This didn't surprise me as Margaret laughed a lot anyway. What did surprise me was her answer: 'I don't care what you do. I like being with you.' The only change in her manner was when she asked me: 'Do you ever hurt people?'

My reply was perfectly natural: 'Never! I abhor violence!'

Later, there would come a time, sitting in a prison cell, when those words would come back to haunt me.

'Now I have something to tell you,' she said, touching her stomach. 'The father of this child, he's an Irish police-man.' There was a certain sense of irony here.

'That's OK,' I said, 'I won't blame the child.' We both laughed, with a sense of relief. Now, we knew each other's secrets.

With Margaret in my trust, it was possible to make some kind of provision for her. I bought her an expensive gold charm bracelet. At least once a month, I would buy another charm to be added to it. I told her the saleable value of each piece. If I was behind bars, the dangling bits of gold would feed her and her child. I also made sure that she always had £500 in her handbag.

It was on a late autumn afternoon that my forage around my landlady's caravan started to bear fruit. Margaret, now heavily pregnant, was cooking. I was sitting at the kitchen table nursing a brandy. We were chatting easily, the way that couples do. I noticed Mrs Nielsen's head, occasionally bobbing past the open window as she went about gardening chores. I knew that she was listening to us. I started telling Margaret about some imaginary land that I had been given information about.

This land had aroused the interest of a famous garage conglomerate. My plan was to buy quickly, hold on to it for a couple of months, and then sell, at a huge profit. Lost amidst thoughts of her baby's impending birth and the meal she was preparing, she responded only with ums and ahs.

Out in the garden, I noticed that Mrs Nielsen's movements had almost completely ceased. There are numerous things that I have observed about human nature. One of them is that a lot of people stand still when they listen. Later that evening, our landlady came up to the house to see me. She casually mentioned that she had a pound or two in the bank that wasn't earning much. Did I, as a businessman, have any advice for her, on how the money could be put to better use? I asked her how much she would like to invest.

The next day she gave me a cheque for £1,000. Telling

her that the money was invested, I started paying her a weekly interest rate of £20. In 1965, this was more than the average weekly wage. She was drawn in.

It was approaching Christmas when Margaret gave birth to a beautiful baby girl, Caroline. I showered the both of them with expensive gifts. I hired a Rolls Royce to bring Margaret back from the nursing home I'd booked her into. To all outward appearances, we now looked like some archetypal, middle-class, country family.

Mrs Nielsen cooed over young Caroline. She also asked whether she could invest some more money. I said: 'Certainly, how much were you thinking of?' As she sat in front of our log fire, drinking my Scotch – for which she had a huge appetite – she contemplated the sum. She signed the cheque, then carrying on drinking, seemed to forget.

When, slightly drunk, she tottered off to the end of the garden, the cheque lay on my coffee table, her signature at the bottom, the amount left blank. Again, my earlier forage in her home paid dividends. I knew more or less what her assets were. I filled in the blank space – £12,350. I would leave her with a couple of thousand pounds in the account, just to avoid raising suspicions.

Mrs Nielsen's bank was opposite mine in Tunbridge Wells. I was in no doubt that, in a small town such as this, the two managers would be friendly. I would have to play this very carefully.

I held off banking the cheque until just before the close of business on Tuesday. For the next three days I half expected a call of some kind, questioning what I was doing with my landlady's life savings. None came. On the Friday, the day before Nielsen's cheque would clear, I visited my bank. I told the manager that I was going to buy some land from a local farmer. The only thing was, the farmer would only take cash. If I was to pop in on the Saturday morning, would there be enough money available for me to make a £15,000 withdrawal. Again, I would leave a couple of hundred in the account, just to allay suspicions. He told me there would be no problem.

My initial fear was that my landlady's banker would question why almost all of her savings were being transferred into my account across the road. If this happened, I would have to cut and run. I couldn't afford questions being asked about me. My luck seemed to be in, the cheque had obviously escaped his attention, and was now in the system. Now, I had one more day to go. I had to make sure that Nielsen didn't visit her bank or, if she did, I had to know about it. At 9.30am, briefcase in hand, I went to my bank and withdrew her money. I got back to the farm as quickly as possible. I wanted to know her movements. She went out in her van delivering eggs. I followed at a discreet distance.

In the village, she called at the post office and, in a twenty-yard walk that took years off my life, went straight past her bank. When she arrived back at the farm I urged Margaret to engage her in conversation, and do whatever she had to do to keep her there. It was now 10.50am. Ten more minutes. On an instinct I called Mrs Nielsen's bank, and asked them what time they closed. The reply was 11.30am.

I spent the next forty minutes asking my soon-to-be-exlandlady every conceivable question about her life, farming, her politics. As long as the old bag stood there chatting, I was going to be quids in. The minutes passed by. At 11.25am, myself, Margaret, my landlady and I all stood in the farmyard, drinking hot toddies, made with Mrs Nielsen's favourite Scotch whisky – mine. As I said to her at the time: 'It's a cold day and what the hell.'

I've no doubt that the reason Mrs Nielsen enjoyed drinking my Scotch wasn't so much the taste, but more that she considered it to be 'free'. If I was to calculate how much Scotch I gave her, and how much money I took off her, each glass, and I'm guessing there were sixty, would have cost her around £240. If she had known the price, I doubt whether she would have beamed at me so appreciatively every time I gave her a refill.

When the appointed hour had been and gone, I decided to stop standing in a windy farmyard, talking shit to an old lady who bored me to death. The briefcase full of money was hidden in one of the outhouses, under logs cut for the fire. I told Margaret to get Caroline and her coat. We were going shopping.

Before I started spending real money, I laid the groundwork for one more scam. There's no point going to all the hard work of earning trust in the community if you don't rip them off before vanishing. I called in at the jewellers. As you can imagine, with my past, this was a shop I had been in many times. Margaret's expensive charms had been bought here. I was a valued and trusted customer.

I told the manager that I wished to buy an expensive watch, two gold cigarette cases, a gold bracelet, plus more charms for Margaret's bracelet. Saying that I would think about it, I left the shop without buying anything. If I hadn't bought anything there, we more than made up for it in the rest of the shops. Gifts for Caroline, gifts for Margaret, gifts for myself. Clothes for all of us. We bought so much that we had to hire a taxi to follow us home with the parcels and bags.

Back at the farm, we lit a roaring fire and I started to set the scene for the next part of my plan. I laid out wads of banknotes on the mantelpiece, bottles of drink adorned the coffee table. The room was strikingly festive. Just as I knew the jewellers would be closing, I phoned. I told him that I'd been thinking about the pieces I'd looked at earlier in the day. I'd decided to buy them. Would he mind terribly bringing them out to the house? He replied: 'Of course, Mr Philips.' He knew that it was worthwhile. Fifteen minutes later, the jeweller arrived. Sitting him down close to the fire, I offered him a pre-Christmas drink, a large tumbler full of fine brandy. He accepted and we chatted. As fast as his drink emptied, Margaret refilled it. The room was hot, he was relaxed and, now feeling the effects of the drink, I saw his eyes take in the sizable amount of cash, just seemingly laying around. 'Would you prefer cash or cheque?' I asked him. Everything in that room, told him that I was a man of means. 'Whichever is best for you' was his reply. Casually, I took out my cheque book. He had been conned.

As soon as we had waved him off, we started packing. We drove to London where, after booking Margaret and the baby into a hotel, I returned to the farm to collect the

147

luggage we couldn't manage on the first trip. As I walked out of the house with more suitcases, Mrs Nielsen peered through the window of her caravan. I called to her. 'We're just having a few days' break.' I watched as her lined face broke into a smile and she raised her glass to me. Putting the suitcases in the car, I raised my hand in a wave: 'Merry Christmas, Mrs Nielsen.' She never saw me again.

The next day, my new family and I headed for Wales. We spent Christmas in the Angel Hotel, Cardiff. From there we moved on to Caerphilly, where we enjoyed the sights of mid-Glamorgan and saw out the year. The calendar moved on to 1966.

Caroline was a lovely young child, but a life of moving from hotel to hotel, rented house to rented house was no life for a young baby. Youngsters need stability, a home that they know and where they feel secure. I talked to Margaret. She loved her child, but she didn't want to lose me. She had no means of support, so how would she live if she was left alone to bring up a child on State benefits? Also, Margaret was becoming accustomed to the good life. She enjoyed being a criminal's girlfriend. I knew of a very, very good friend whose wife absolutely adored children. A natural earth mother. I phoned her, she agreed to take the baby for a few months. Margaret and I would just 'take it on the lamb'. Although I was as careful as I could be, I was an active thief who had escaped from prison. As such, my photograph was in every police station in the country. It could all end at any minute. I had considered living in Wales, but after going there, decided against it.

Instead, we moved to a seafront bungalow in Weston-super-Mare. Going abroad was in our minds at that time, but for that I would need a large 'score'. No point going to live in the sunshine, if you've got to work for a living. The sunshine, and a life outside Britain, never happened. What did happen, four days after moving in, was that a well-dressed man, wearing a milkman's jacket, knocked on the front door early one Monday morning. I had been shaving in the bathroom, and answered it with soap still on my face. Holding two pints in his hand, the milkman asked me how much milk we wanted. I said: 'Whatever my wife has ordered.' I called Margaret, who shouted back: 'Two pints.' With a sense of dread, I closed the door. As I walked back to the bathroom, I commented to Margaret that our milkman had taken to wearing a suit and tie beneath his overjacket. Looking through the bathroom window I saw them: plain clothes, uniforms, cars. Wiping my face, I waited for the inevitable.

When George, Don and I had trouble crossing the river after our breakout, I remember thinking that I would rather drown than be recaptured. Once the other two had been taken, I had bought myself a revolver and bullets, ready for the day when they would try to put me back into a prison cell. What I had not taken into account was that I would have a young woman to care for. If I opened fire, what would happen to Margaret?

The next time someone knocked on the door, I wasn't expecting a well-dressed coalman. Nor was I disappointed. Two plain clothes detectives stepped into the hallway. After showing me their identification they told me that they had reason to believe that I was Roy Hall, aka Roy Fontaine. With a dozen policemen surrounding me I was taken into custody.

I had various types of identification, driving licence, cheque book, passport, all in the name of Philips. But the police had my prints, and photographs. Margaret denied all knowledge of my activities and was released. I was allowed a phone call. I called John Wooton, who drove through the night and, picking up Margaret, took her to Stafford to live with him and my mother.

While they drove north, I sat in a police cell in Weston-super-Mare, and waited for detectives from Edinburgh, who were flying down to question me. Weeks of custody ensued, and detectives came from all over. I was questioned again and again. I admitted nothing but was charged with everything. At Edinburgh High Court I was found guilty of numerous cases of theft and fraud. The judge gave me five years but, in his sentencing, he omitted the word 'consecutive' which meant the smaller sentence of five would be swallowed by the larger eight, the remainder of my earlier sentence of ten years. Once again, I walked down the dock steps to prison life.

14

A SITUATION IS WHAT YOU MAKE OF IT

First stop this time was Aberdeen. A cold, bleak place where I was forced to make fishing nets in a tin shed. My hands would be numb and my body would shake with the cold. I was a high-risk prisoner and, as such, didn't qualify for any of the decent jobs. I sensed 'hard time' in front of me. If I thought my life was piss poor, it didn't compare to that of a young prisoner on my wing. He was an attractive young man, heterosexual, with a young wife and baby. This was his first time behind bars. Such people can be easy prey. One night, I heard his muffled screams, as six men gang-raped him. His cries of helpless torment did nothing to stop his rapists' lust.

I have had sex with many men, outside prison and inside, but always consenting. The cries of a rape victim live inside your head for many a long day. If I had had my gun, the first scream I heard would have been the last. The scum that fucked his arse would have died on the spot.

Early one freezing morning, under heavy escort, I was transferred to Durham. They put me in the isolation block. After a few days I was moved again, this time to Wandsworth. I'd no sooner settled into my cell, when they told me to pack again. This was the move I had dreaded – Parkhurst. I was going back to the island. Of all the prisons I've been in, and I've been in many, Parkhurst is without doubt the shittiest, most soul-destroying place imaginable. My worst fears were about to be realised. Besides finding myself back in the worst nick, I was again an 'E' man and subject to a more stringent regime than the ordinary men. Parkhurst was full of 'faces'. With the country's top thieves and most feared gangsters within its walls, Parkhurst was a fearful place to be. Before my time was through, I would experience brutality like never before. If I became a murderer, then some of the officers there should hold their hands up and say: 'We helped to shape him into what he was.'

I had regular visits from Margaret. Some cons commented on how lucky I was to have a young girlfriend travelling all that way to see me, lucky to have someone so devoted. I wasn't being cynical when I said it wouldn't last. On one visit, I told her that she had no future with me. I still had a few years to do and she should meet someone younger and honest. Someone rich, if possible, and start a new life. That day she left the prison in tears. It was a hard thing for me to say. When your life is a living hell, the outside contact gives you the strength to carry on. She continued to write, but gradually the letters became less frequent. Then, out of the blue, she asked for a visiting order. She came to see me, but it was to say goodbye. She had met an Arab, and together with his family, was emigrating to Canada. I hugged her and wished her all the happiness in the world. I had never been in love with her, but her vulnerability evoked the part of me that is tender and caring. How she touched my soul, I will never know. What I do know is that the side of me that Margaret brought forth is the side that I felt happiest with. Even a man like myself realises such things.

They say that like attracts like. If Parkhurst had the worst criminals, it most certainly had the worst screws. Corruption in prisons is a fact of life. Warders make money trading for the cons. Generally this suits all concerned, but sometimes the greed of men becomes too much and breeds resentment.

There was a warder in Parkhurst who embodied all that is worst about prison corruption. He would deal with the cons, but his prices were extortionate. If you are going to make money out of prisoners, you should treat them fairly in other respects. It should have been a case of 'you scratch my back, and I'll scratch yours'. But this man was a hypocrite. He had no regard for the system he worked for and he would break every prison rule in order to line his own nest. Then, once the deal had been done, he would turn. He worked extra shifts in the punishment block through choice. He loved to taunt and provoke prisoners. When on exercise, he would change the clock, cutting down the time that should have been allowed to cons.

When you returned he would have pulled the old trick of placing live matches in the cracks in your cell floor. The con would be put on another charge. If you dared to complain, you felt his stick and boot. The trade that this greedy, sadistic bastard engaged in was itself unusual. For a price, and I mean hundreds of pounds, he would alter your prison records. You could buy sheets of your own past. This meant a con could have his worst offences vanish into thin air, when the parole board looked at his papers. A few cons, those with the necessary cash, started to do business with him. These were almost exclusively high-risk prisoners. Eventually it was my turn. We talked, I paid, he gave me a sheet from my record. I should have been happy, but the beatings he gave out, his sadistic pleasure at seeing others suffer, was hard to swallow. A few of us talked, and we decided that we wanted to get rid of him. We decided to inform the Governor about him. To turn in someone who can bring your release date closer might seem strange, but hate and fear are powerful emotions. Our only weapon against him was his own corruption.

I made an application to see the Governor. I told the boss that I had heard disturbing rumours about cons' records being tampered with. I dared not give a name. Other 'E' men did the same thing, again, no names, but the fingers were all pointing in one direction. These complaints were waived. Frustrated at the lack of action, I again put in a request to see the Governor. Again, the complaint was waived. When I put in a third request, I went prepared. In a re-run of the previous visits, I voiced my concern that prisoners' records were being tampered with and were for sale. The Governor lost his temper: 'We've been through all this before. Your accusations are completely unfounded.' Putting my hand inside my shirt front, I pulled out two pages of my prison record. I tossed them on to his desk: 'Then perhaps you could explain to me how these are in my possession?' I still refused to give a name, but I knew he suspected the right man. Bound by procedure, he was forced to act.

A few days later, the local police started to interview us. All told, there were about twelve of us involved. If we knew that the investigation was above board, we would have screamed his name from the rooftops, but we were unsure of these detectives. The Isle of Wight is a small place, the police used the prison officers' social club and they all drank together. If we gave a name and then they buried the information and told the screw involved, we could expect severe recriminations.

As if reading our thoughts, a detective and sergeant came to visit us at the prison. All twelve cons were present. The detective asked us whether we watched the six o'clock news on TV, we replied that we did. 'Well, if you watch tonight, you'll see that we are doing our job. If there are bad things happening in this prison, and we uncover them, we will prosecute.' That evening we rushed expectantly to take our seats in the TV room. True to the detective's word, we watched a police car draw up to the warder's house and, seconds later, he was taken away under arrest.

The atmosphere at Parkhurst now became electric. Prisoners were offered help with their parole dates, if they would give information that would help the arrested screw.

Needless to say, nobody did. Sadists don't elicit much sympathy. Under heavy escort the twelve of us were taken to Newport Magistrates' court. One by one we stood in the dock and told our story. The officer was committed to stand trial at Winchester Crown Court.

In the background of all this activity, something else had happened. Information about corruption in Parkhurst had reached the media. A young up-and-coming journalist called Paul Foot visited the prison. As events unfolded, information was passed to him. An article about corruption in Parkhurst was published in *Private Eye*. While the public read, those of us who had testified were taken from our cells and put into the segregation unit. Some officers whispered into our ears and dug us with their truncheons. We were told we were going to 'pay' for this. However, with the trial date coming up they didn't dare damage our faces.

Those of us who had put ourselves on the line were anxious. If the warder was reinstated, we would be facing the wrath of every truncheon-happy screw in the prison. The detective in charge of the case told us not to worry. He was sure the case was sound. The day before the trial, he returned to the prison with the news that the judge had changed. So had the prosecutor. Both were overtly Establishment figures and the Prison Officers Association had paid for a top QC to defend their man.

The defence's main argument was that prisoners didn't have money. If they didn't have money, how could they possibly pay this man to remove their records? It was nothing more than an elaborate plot by a few high-risk

A SITUATION IS WHAT YOU MAKE OF IT

prisoners to get themselves transferred to a less austere prison on the mainland.

Anybody with any knowledge of prison life knows that this is rubbish. Money is used on the inside as much as it is on the outside. The only difference is that people on the outside put it in a wallet, and prisoners stick it up their arses. There are men walking around today who, if you made them shit on camera, would produce enough money to make you think it was a lottery win.

The top detective on the case spoke to me in an interview room at the court. He knew that the defence's argument was ludicrous. He also knew of the political shenanigans of the Home Office. As he finished speaking to me, he dropped something on the floor. Without looking back, he left the room. I picked up the paper, it was a £10 note.

Back in the courtroom I was put on the stand. The defence counsel's inference that I was an inveterate liar was immensely irritating. After hearing my testimony being ridiculed yet again, I spoke once more. 'It seems that whatever I say, you are not prepared to give me the benefit of the doubt.' Reaching into my breast jacket pocket, I produced the banknote. 'Perhaps, this will speak more eloquently than any words I might say.' I held the note up for the judge to see. I heard him say: 'Am I to understand that this is a Treasury note?' The clerk of the court came over to me and, taking it, gave it to the Judge for closer inspection. If prisoners didn't have money, what the fuck was this? The court fell silent.

The jury was out for eight hours. When they came back in, they returned a verdict of not guilty.

THE WICKED MR HALL

That evening, the twelve of us who had taken the stand were moved to Winchester. The atmosphere was very grim. Again, we were all placed in segregation. That first night, the beatings started. We had dared to challenge their supposedly unassailable authority. The whispered threats of Parkhurst became reality.

When they came, it was in the middle of the night. The cell door would crash open. Six, sometimes more, would charge. In front of them, they would carry a mattress just in case their intended victim was ready to defend himself. Once they were on you, the mattress would be tossed to one side. Blows from riot sticks would rain down on your body, their clamouring hands would grab your testicles and squeeze. The pain of this alone could make a man lose consciousness. Their heavy boots would kick and kick and kick. Broken noses, black eyes and bruises and weals which would cover your body from head to toe. Each of us was visited. The sound of the screams would carry from one end of the wing to the other. I don't know which was worse, being the subject of the beating yourself or hearing the screams of your friends. I still can feel it, I still can hear it.

One by one, we all started being moved out to other prisons. In the end, I was the only one left. I had been considered the ringleader. I wondered what my fate would be. These men wanted to kill us.

At 6.00am one morning, three screws came into my cell and told me to pack up my belongings. While I dressed, they started breaking my few personal possessions – my radio, my thermos flask. If it was breakable they smashed it before flinging the shattered remains into a box. I was supposed to be taken to reception but, instead, I was marched to a stripped cell. There was no bed, no furniture, just blankets covering the floor. Warders with truncheons lined the walls. I was ordered to lay down. I did as I was told, I closed my eyes and waited for the beating to commence. But none came. After a few minutes, they filed out of the cell, laughing. It had just been a game. Intimidation. An amusing way for them to pass the drudgery of their long night shift.

I was bundled, handcuffed, into the back of a prison van. With police cars at the front and rear, and motorcycle riders to our left and right, we started to go north. Where were they taking me? We stopped for lunch in Wakefield. I thought that was it, but the journey continued. It was mid-afternoon before I realised that Hull was my destination.

15

A STOLEN HEART

At that time, Hull was a long-termer's prison. A couple of the Great Train Robbers were there, one of whom, Jimmy Hussey, became my friend. The Lambrianou brothers, the Kray twins' henchmen, were also on the wing. The Governor was a man called Bill Perry, big in stature and big in every other kind of way. A fair and just man, the prison reflected his own personality. There was an attitude of give and take between the inmates and staff. The day after my arrival I was taken to see him. He told me that what was past was past. There was no discernible corruption in his prison, and the beating of prisoners wasn't allowed. After the memory of that morning, lying on the blanketed floor, waiting for hell, I breathed a sigh of relief. Never has the old saying 'What a difference a day makes' had more meaning.

The other cons on the wing were good types. None of us

courted trouble and none came our way. A small group of us would sit together at lunchtime. We would share the cost of sauces and small luxuries that make institutionalised food more palatable. When one of our group was to be discharged, the warder asked us who we would like to join us. Ours was a well-run wing.

A few day's previously, a young man had arrived at the prison. He was high-risk like myself, doing eighteen years for armed robberies and shooting a policeman in London. We sensed we would like him. He was invited on to our wing and on to our table. His name was David Barnard. His introduction into my life would cause me much joy and, eventually, incredible heartbreak.

Dave had the cell next to mine and, with the free time that we had, more and more of it was spent together. For a young man serving such a sentence, his attitude was very mature. Almost immediately, we felt a sense of ease with each other that can sometimes take years to achieve. We liked the same kinds of music. I would write, he would read. If there was silence, it was a relaxed, comfortable quiet. What had initially been a liking developed into a strong affection. It felt good to have this close human contact. At times, a prison can be the loneliest place on earth. My cell almost became like our little home. In the evening Dave would cook us a nice chicken or suchlike, and we would have a couple of glasses of wine together before lock-up. That was something else the prosecution at Winchester Crown Court would have had trouble believing.

As time went by, his feelings and mine sought fuller expression. It was he who spoke. We were sitting alone in my cell one evening when he awkwardly broached the subject. He told me that he had formed a great affection for someone inside the prison, but he was frightened to speak as the affection that he spoke of went beyond the realms of ordinary friendship. I asked him who it was. He said that he didn't want to say, that if he was truthful about his feelings, it might destroy the relationship. I replied that if one person spoke honestly to another, how could it destroy anything? If it did, then it was nothing in the first place. I urged him to tell me: 'If you can't speak to him, let me.' In my heart of hearts, I dreaded hearing any other name but my own. After a short silence he said: 'The man I'm speaking of is the man I'm speaking to.' I looked at him. I felt more love for this human being than I had for any other, before or since. I told him to close the door. We made love. In the past, the sex that I'd had with men was purely lust. The feelings and the sensations with Dave Barnard were on a different plane. I would have laid down my life for this man. Just to be with him, just to look at him, made me feel whole. After that, we were an 'item'. At the age of forty-six, I finally understood what it was to be in love.

John Wooton continued to be the true friend that he had always been. He made sure that I was never short of money. I managed to get myself a canary that mated with another con's bird. I gave the chick to Dave. Then I transformed my cell into a place where a man could live with some dignity. Red curtains, red carpet, red bedspread – colour gives warmth and hope. I hung a picture of the boy King Tutankhamun on one wall.

THE WICKED MR HALL

I can be a cynical man. In my life I have experienced broken promises and dashed expectations. When this happens, you build a wall, a protective shield. When hungry you eat, when lustful you gratify yourself. The base emotions are easy to deal with, but what of love? It is natural to question. There were times when I questioned. Did Dave love me? Did I love him? Was this feeling real or would it vanish into the ether like a child's dream? I was given the answer when Dave argued with, and then threatened, a screw. He was put on a charge and moved to the punishment block. The core of my life had been taken from me. First, I just missed him. Each second, each minute, each hour, seemed to stretch into an eternity. After the yearning, the longing just to see him and hear his voice, came the anger. I started to seethe inside. Because of some screw, I no longer felt complete, I was no longer whole. There is a side of me, when aroused, that is cold and completely heartless. That uniformed bastard had crossed the line. He was on dangerously thin ice.

The next day, I saw him. I was carrying a scalding hot pot of tea up a staircase. He was there, smiling. His life was intact. I wanted to see him scream, I wanted his face to burn. I removed the lid from the pot then, positioning myself, readied to sling it into his face. A con, a friend, slapped my arm as the scalding brown liquid started its journey from metal container to flesh. The tea sprayed harmlessly on to the concrete floor. There was no injury, but the intent was clear. Now I was on a charge and I joined Dave in the punishment block. As I was taken down, I heard one screw say to another: 'I told you it wouldn't be long till Roy got here.' The warders compassionately allowed Dave and myself to exercise at the same time. One hour out of every twenty-four could be spent with him. It was worth the loss of privileges. I would have walked through fire for David Barnard. After that, there was no more questioning. I loved him. There is no emotion so powerful.

For the first time in my life, I considered going straight. My release date would come first. I would gather the necessary capital and, when Dave walked out of prison, we would go legit. We would open a club or restaurant or something along those lines. This was a completely new way of thinking for me. It was also a nice feeling – a future, without the police chasing me, and without the threat of being locked up again. The change in our attitude was noticed. A warder commented on how much calmer Dave seemed nowadays. I was taken off the 'E' list.

Prison life continued to roll along its weary course. The weeks turned into months and, one Wednesday morning, the Governor sent for me. My first parole date was in the near future. He was going to recommend me for release. He didn't see me as any choirboy, but he thought that I was a man of some principle, who, if he wanted it bad enough, was capable of leading a worthwhile and law-abiding life. I assured him that, at my age, I had had enough. I was thoroughly sick of going from prison term to prison term. I told him of my plans for a future with Dave. He was pleased that the years had mellowed me and that my days of being a menace to society were, at last, coming to an end.

I set about increasing my chances in front of the parole board. If you take educational courses in prison, the information goes into your file. If you apply for jobs on the outside, it goes into your file. The more moves you make, the better it looks. I made ninety-four moves, ninety-four letters to different companies and establishments. None of them as a butler. I wrote to Sir John Cohen, head of Tesco. I wrote to Hugh Frazer, the man who gambled and lost control of Harrods. The secretary to Lord Rank, the film magnate, wrote back to me, saying that if I could give him a definite date of release, he would do all he could to help me. I went about the idea of building a new life with all the fervour that I had previously put into thieving. I made phonecalls, I did my research and not only did I write to company premises, I wrote to people's home addresses. My efforts were duly noted by the prison authorities and in the winter of 1970 I was given my parole date, subject to spending eight months in a prison hostel in Preston, Lancashire.

The first thing you want to do when you enter a prison is leave. All of my working life, this had been a constant. I had jumped from a moving train to avoid prison, I had crawled over roofs, scaled barbed wire fences, I had almost frozen to death, I had rolled out of a first-floor hospital window, I had sat in my own piss.

All for freedom!

And now, just as it was being given to me, I no longer knew that I wanted it. Of course, I did want it, but, I wanted it with Dave. There are many kinds of freedom. There is freedom to walk the streets, freedom to shape your own destiny, freedom to die, if that is your wish. Dave Barnard had already given me a type of freedom. It was freedom from loneliness. Wherever I was, inside or out, if he wasn't there that freedom was taken away. This was a quandary like no other. We talked and talked and talked. Other prisoners urged me to take the parole, saying I could do more for Dave on the outside. None of them truly understood. For Dave, it was truly awful. He loved me, he wanted me to be free, but he didn't want to lose me. In the end, his love proved to be unconditional – if I went, I could start to lay the first bricks of our future. At 8.00am one Saturday, I stepped free of the prison gates of Hull. It was with a mixture of relief and heartbreak that I got onto the Preston-bound train.

On arrival in Preston, I hailed a taxi and asked him to take me to the nearest newsagents. I looked through his stock and bought every magazine that I thought Dave might like. From there I went to a record shop and bought him some of his favourite music. With the taxi fare still ticking, we drove to the Post Office where I parcelled it all up and sent if off to Hull. I did all this, even before reporting to the hostel. From now on gifts and letters would be my only link with him. It gave me great satisfaction.

Prison hostels are not nice places. One is much like the other. You are allowed out from eight in the morning till ten at night. You must attend whichever job they find for you, and you share a room with two or three other men. Preston was, it must be said, quite well run. This was largely due to a Mr Burser, a Polish man, who was the principal warder. Burser was intelligent and orderly. We got on rather well and he was kind to me in many ways and, because of him, my stay there was tolerable. I had little time for contact with my roommates. They were a very poor type whose main source of interest was visits to the pub. They seemed to lack intelligence and ambition. This didn't bother me, the only thing I did there was sleep.

The morning after my arrival, a prison officer took me on a short tour of the town. Notorious pubs, which I was told to avoid, were pointed out to me. We stopped at the police station car park, where I was asked to get out of the car. Looking at the blue lamps and notices that said 'Police', I was told: 'This is the police station, we don't want you to give them any reason to talk to you.' In the second storey windows, I saw detectives' faces peering through the glass. This was the reason I was standing here, the local plain clothes had requested a look at me. After this most unusual identification parade, I was taken to what was to be my new place of work.

Whittingham Hospital was an institution for the insane, a couple of miles outside the town. The hospital had a policy of employing two hostel men each year. After being interviewed by the catering manager, I was told that I was to work as a kitchen porter. The wages and work were menial and abysmal. It didn't matter, I still had access to money and I still had my wits. I would turn this situation around. One thing that had turned to my advantage was that John Wooton and my mother had left Stafford, and settled in nearby Lytham St Annes. My old partner was only twelve miles away.

A STOLEN HEART

On my first day at work, a 33-year-old Irish waitress from Belfast came over and introduced herself to me. The fact that I had just been released from prison seemed to make me all the more attractive to her. She liked criminals. That afternoon, I had sex with her in one of the rooms. This was my first meeting with Mary Coggles.

Opposite the prison was a pub called The Crown. I soon established a habit of calling in there at about 9.45pm for my last brandy of the day. I became friendly with the landlord, who got to know of my situation. Under hostel rules, I wasn't allowed to have a car, but, without a vehicle I felt completely lost, and I hated using public transport. I had talked to John on the phone and, using some funds of mine that he was holding, he bought me a Rover. I explained the hostel rules to the pub landlord, and he gave me permission to use his car park. Slowly, things were looking up.

From the first time that I'd slept with Mary Coggles, I knew what I wanted from her. In the right clothes, and after a visit to the hairdresser, her cheerful personality would make her the perfect prison visitor for Dave. At that time, ex-convicts were not allowed to visit the prison from which they had just been released. After buying her some nice outfits and covering all expenses, I started using Mary as a go-between. She would smuggle him letters, presents and my love. Considering that I was sleeping with her, I thought this quite broad-minded of her.

As Dave's family had completely abandoned him, I encouraged John, my mother, Mary and other friends to write him regular letters. If people went on holiday, I urged them to send him postcards. Besides living in the hostel and working at the mental hospital, another parole condition was that every two weeks I had to report to a probation officer. This man was very easy to manipulate. As soon as I felt I had gained his trust, I started bringing him presents of bottles of whisky, which he gratefully recieved. I persuaded him to write letters supporting Dave's case for early release. Although my working days were busy and my social life improving, the energy and drive behind everything was still Dave Barnard. I wanted him free.

Spending any more time in the hostel than I needed to was unthinkable. John and my mother made regular visits, always taking me to nice restaurants and clubs. The unoccupied nights were soon filled by the RAF club a stone's throw from the prison gates. The clientele there was slightly more upmarket, and it was here that I first met Hazel Paterson. Loud, large and blonde, she sat on a stool at the bar. I was already on nodding terms with her, as she owned the general store/newsagents where I bought my morning paper. I introduced myself, and immediately sensed that she was interested. The person I loved, I couldn't see. Mary was just someone to have sex with, who I used to pass messages to Dave. This shopowner seemed to be a woman of some wealth. She was also lonely, and I was ready for some diversification.

One night, as I prepared to leave the club, she said, 'You're like Cinderella, always vanishing at the same time.' I told her that I was going to the desolate grey building just down the road. 'Oh, you work there?' 'No, I don't work there. I live there, I'm a prisoner on licence.' She seemed surprised, but not put off by this. Smiling, she invited me to visit her more often at her shop. This was fine by me, in fact it was exactly what I wanted to happen.

Hazel was the widow of a Lancashire publisher. Her money had come from her dead husband. As far as business acumen went, she didn't have much. Although the lounge was only a few feet away from the counter area, the door was always closed. While Hazel passed away her days, the two young girls who worked for her were left in charge of the money. After a couple of visits, I persuaded her to keep the door open and, with the help of two carefully positioned mirrors, she could sit and watch what her hired help was up to. The takings rose considerably. After that, she was very open to my advice. I had gained her trust.

I started having sex with her – more because I thought she expected it of me than from any great lust on my part. She liked us to do it in a heavily perfumed bath. I performed adequately but afterwards, as I showered, I was left with a feeling of unfulfilment. For me, this relationship was devoid of love. Hazel Paterson and her home were just a nice diversion from spending time in a lowlife hostel.

However, that was not how she saw it, and it was not to my credit that I didn't tell her the truth. This act of selfishness would later boomerang on me.

She talked of selling the shop, and I encouraged her. Through sheer chance, I found myself alone one day with the prospective buyer. He was complaining that she was dragging her feet. Due to other commitments, he wanted a quick deal. I listened to him and went to see him the following day. I asked him: 'What would it be worth to you, if I could get Hazel out of the shop within seven days?' After some contemplation, he replied: 'A couple of hundred quid.' I disagreed: 'No, no, no. This place is a little goldmine. The takings for each week are in the thousands. It sells every conceivable thing, it's ideally situated on a busy thoroughfare.' Standing up, I said, 'Think about it, I'll call in again tomorrow.' The next day, he agreed to a sum of £800. Within a week, Hazel was out, he was in and my wallet was full of money.

Apart from me having to leave early, our social life was quite interesting. Hazel was well connected to all the local dignitaries. She was a friend of the Mayor, and together we would attend most of the civic functions. Hazel was keen to get a car. I knew of a doctor at the hospital, who was selling his Jaguar, and I put her in touch with him. One night after returning from work, I went into the kitchen, and noticed a brown envelope on the table, addressed to me. Inside were the log book and keys to the Jag. She had bought it for me. Also, the proceeds from the sale of the shop had been put into a joint bank account. I had access to thousands of pounds again, and two cars. For someone earning £20 a week and living inside prison grounds, this was quite a remarkable feat. Life at the hospital was also improving. I had developed quite a rapport with the catering manager, and my duties had changed. Along with Mary Coggles, I had taken charge of the VIP suite and on one occasion even served dinner to Sir Keith Joseph, the Health Minister.

When the mood took me, I still had sex with Mary.

Besides her, I branched out and started sleeping with a young chef called Tony. Whittingham hospital wasn't that bad after all! As I always say: 'A situation is what you make it.'

I was invited to a party in London by Patrick Rafferty, a criminal friend from Hull Prison. It was there that I met the only woman I was ever to love, the only woman I would ever marry. Ruth Holmes. I still loved David. Is it possible to love two people at once? Yes!

Ruth worked for one of the city's big fashion houses. She was elegance personified – her clothes, her bearing, her manner. She stole my heart. I stole hers by sending a restaurant waiter out to the car to serve her a drink while we were waiting for take-away food. It happened in an instant. As with Dave, when we made love, 'love' really was one of the factors. I started to spend my weekends in London.

I was now approaching the end of my time at the hospital and I was asked whether I would like to stay on as one of the Dining Managers. I thanked them for their kind offer, and said I'd consider it. In truth, it was completely out of the question but, until my parole had officially ended, I dared not show my hand to anyone. The last few weeks in Preston weren't that difficult to bear. I kept up my pretence of being Hazel's partner. At the hospital I was still sleeping with Mary and the chef and, as a bonus, I was having an illicit affair with a young woman from Blackpool, who was my half-brother Donald's girlfriend. Come the end of the week, it was back to London and Ruth. It was a bitch of a job, having sex with all those different people but then I suppose someone had to do it.

THE WICKED MR HALL

The long eight-month period of sleeping from Monday to Friday in the bleak hostel finally came to an end. I made a rather substantial withdrawal from my and Hazel's bank account, and left. Preston was a definite backnumber. Northern mill towns have never quite been my cup of tea.

Ruth and myself had a quiet registry office wedding and I moved into her spacious Hammersmith flat.

I had been careful to keep various compartments of my life separate. Ruth knew nothing of what had been happening in Preston. Hazel Paterson knew nothing of Mary Coggles, who I was still using to visit Dave in Hull. And Mary, who was a simple soul, had been told to keep her mouth shut. I had carefully and quietly swapped one life for another. Ruth saw me as a slightly unscrupulous businessman, which, I suppose, if applied in its loosest sense, was almost true.

Grimshaw Hall was a manor house in Knowle, Warwickshire, set in three hundred acres of undulating countryside, with peacocks roaming the gardens. It boasted a huge indoor swimming-pool. The old riding stables had been converted into a suite of luxurious offices. A fleet of expensive cars sat in the garages – Rolls, Lamborghinis, sports cars. The owner of this private paradise was a man named Angelo Southall, a multi-millionaire who had advertised for a butler. Telling Ruth that I was going to do some business deals in that area, I took the job. The only person I trusted with the truth was John Wooton. I phoned him once a week, and told people to contact me through him. When I had told the Governor of Hull that I was sick of prison, I had been telling the truth. Although now married, my plans for Dave and myself going into business were still in my mind. This time, though, I would take no chances. I would be very careful, and any stones that I took would be replaced with fakes. Nobody would know my whereabouts, I would use an assumed name and I would be in and out in a few weeks. The idea of actually taking a lowly paid job was incomprehensible. With luck, this would be my last criminal foray.

16
IN TOO DEEP

Ruth was wrapped up in her career. After years of giving people stories, I was an expert. She believed the business tale, and our weekends were without strained atmospheres and were full of passion. After all, we were newly-weds. Part of Ruth's attraction for me had been her independence. I had let her know some things from my past. She knew that I had done time, and was aware that I had criminal contacts. Like almost all the women in my life, instead of repulsing it only served to attract them more. A man not willing to have his strings pulled by society was a man in his own right.

We were both relaxing in the flat one Saturday evening when the phone rang. It was an old friend of mine. This particular friend was, I suppose, a gigolo of sorts. He lived the life of a playboy and he was completely immoral. He would sleep with men or women of any age, if they had money or prestige and he could get something from them. He was still relatively young, in his early thirties, and he was very attractive. Down the phone line, he told me the story. He had slept with a very wealthy married man whose wife and children had been away at their country residence. Obviously this man must have some clout, and he was 'in the closet'. On leaving the man's home, he had spotted a briefcase with a huge combination lock on it standing on a hallway table. As he walked out of the front door, he had picked it up. He couldn't open it. It could contain something valuable. Was I interested?

I told him to wait for me and, driving over to his flat, took it from him. I promised him that if it was of use to me, I would give him a fair price. I didn't open it until I was back in the flat with Ruth. What we saw astonished us. The owner of the case was a senior civil servant. Inside were papers, some of which were marked 'One copy only. For the office of the Prime Minister'. There was information on a certain foreign ambassador in London. Other papers related to Dom Mintoff, the Maltese Prime Minister. If this information was leaked, or sold abroad, it would cause the Government acute embarrassment. What I had were confidential Cabinet papers.

Ruth was frightened of the possible consequences, and urged me to burn the papers. But I knew that I would keep them. I couldn't tell my newly-wed wife why. Now I had something that the Government wanted, which was ironic, because the Government had something, or rather someone, I wanted. Dave Barnard. I did some research on the civil servant. Now this was a man who had the ear of the Home Secretary, head of the prison service, the man with the power of veto and release.

The next morning, I went to Euston and made photocopies of all the documents. I posted the copies to John Wooton, telling him to put them in a safe place. From there I went to a public phone box and dialled the number of a Cabinet Minister. The secretary who answered seemed reluctant to put me through until I mentioned that I was in possession of a missing briefcase. Seconds later, I had the ear of the Cabinet Minister. I kept the call as brief as possible. All I wanted to do was establish contact. Half an hour later I called again, this time I was put through straight away. I asked him: 'What are the chances of a prisoner being released in exchange for the briefcase?' He started to procrastinate. I put the phone down. They would already have the necessary equipment in place to instigate a phone trace. I'd let them think about it. Thinking was just what I did, too, when I returned to Ruth's flat. I realised that my initial reaction had been pure 'knee jerk', an emotional response. I wanted the man I loved free. After some thought, it was clear that there was no way I could give them Dave's name, without leading them straight to me. I decided to see what the Russians would offer. Taking some of the least important papers, I visited their Consulate in the Bayswater Road.

After a short wait, I was ushered into an office at the rear of the building. A masculine-type woman, wearing a grey suit and string tie asked what I wanted. I told her that I worked in a government department and, on occasion, came into possession of certain papers. I went on to explain that I felt a friendship towards the Russian people, and would like them to see the documents. I pushed the papers across the desk towards her. After reading them, she picked up the phone and spoke in Russian to what I assumed was a superior. A couple of minutes later, a well-groomed young man came in and indicated that I should follow him.

I was taken up a large marble staircase, and into an office that overlooked the Bayswater Road. There, I repeated my story. I was asked: 'How often do you get such papers?' I said: 'Probably about once a month.' He asked me whether my motives were financial gain. I replied 'No.' Then he asked me whether I would like to visit Russia. To this I replied: 'Yes, very much. I would like to see the Kremlin, the Bolshoi ballet, the Fabergé collection and St Petersburg.' I was assured: 'All of this will be possible, but you must not visit the Consulate again. Everyone who enters the building is photographed.' I was told, at an appointed time the next day, to walk in a certain area of Hyde Park where I would be approached. As I left the building, I wondered if my photograph had just been taken. I knew that I had just stepped out of my depth.

My stroll in the park the next day was hardly relaxing. I walked round and round the same area. Every so often I would sit on one of the benches, but I seemed to be of no interest to anyone. I was actually beginning to think that they had forgotten I was there, when a man approached me. We walked, he talked. He was interested and wanted to see all the papers that I had. He gave me an ex-directory telephone number, which I wrote down on a book of matches that I'd picked up at the bar of the Dorchester. I was to phone this number and an interview would be arranged.

Returning to Grimshaw Hall, I hid the briefcase, along with a revolver and bullets in Southall's wine cellar. My interview with the Russians never happened. I had only been back in Warwickshire for one day, when I telephoned John Wooton for any messages. He told me that Patrick Rafferty had been in touch, and wanted to meet. I called the number that John gave me, and Rafferty said he had some stolen foreign currency and could I help? I said that I could, but because of work commitments I didn't want to travel. Would he come to me? He agreed, and we met in a bar in Solihull. After agreeing a price, I told him that the Hall where I was working was only a fifteen-minute drive away. I would go there, get him the money, and relieve him of his burden. I stood to make a nice profit, but my greed was to prove my undoing. After our business was concluded, he asked me whether I was still in touch with Dave Barnard – Rafferty had been in the same wing as us in Hull. As I drank, my emotions got the better of me, I told him that I'd been doing all I could to get Dave released, including using the top-secret contents of a briefcase to try to cut a deal with the Government. Every single word that I uttered to Rafferty would later rebound on me. As I left him that evening, all my previous caution would count for nothing. The man who had introduced me to my wife, the man I had done dealings with in Hull prison was a 'grass'. My lack of judgement would put me back behind bars. I didn't know it then, but the best days of my life were already over.

Besides giving the police everything he knew on me, Rafferty also made a phone call to Ruth and told her that Dave Barnard was my homosexual lover. At the promptings of the Special Branch, he informed her that it was not a casual relationship, and it wasn't over. The worst kind of enemies are the ones that come disguised as friends.

When I walked into Ruth's flat that weekend, I was greeted by an atmosphere as chilly as the Arctic wind. 'Your friend in Hull prison, Dave. What exactly is your relationship with him?' I knew beyond a shadow of a doubt that someone had told her. I contemplated lying. It would have been easy, but how could I? How could I deny a relationship that was based on something so beautiful as selfless love? I told her the truth. She broke down and cried. Then came a torrent of questions. Had I kissed him? I told her I had. Who was active, and who was passive? I explained that Dave was the passive one. What of the future? 'I've made a promise, that I will meet him when he comes out. We're thinking of starting a business.' After that I left her to contemplate our future. I had dealt her the cruellest blow possible. As for myself, what could I do? I had lived a loveless life for forty-five years then, within the space of eighteen months, I had fallen in love with two people. I also felt cheated. Such is the fickle finger of fate.

I returned to Knowle with a heavy heart.

I was going about my duties in the kitchen when my employer came in: 'Roy, if you see strange people wandering about the grounds don't be alarmed. I have given permission to the local photographic society to come and take some shots of the gardens and birds.' I nodded:

'Very well, Sir.' Unperturbed, I carried on with my work. Within moments, there was a knock on the front door. Expecting an enquiry of some kind from the visitors, I opened it without fear. The two men in front of me showed me identification as they stepped into the hallway. They were Special Branch. My accommodation was a four-bedroomed house situated away from the main house on the far side of the estate, and that is where we went. I have been subject to many interrogations over the years. These men were very professional. They offered me a drink and without me stipulating, they gave me my favourite tipple. Without me mentioning Wooton, they said they would tear his and my mother's house apart if they had to. They would dig up every square inch of Grimshaw Hall, if required. I knew that resistance would only make it harder for me. I led them to the wine cellar and unearthed the briefcase for them. I had forgotten about the gun, that alone meant a five-year sentence. The shit had hit the proverbial fan. I was taken to Paddington Green, the most secure police station in London. All of my belongings followed, every suit I had worn, every scrap of paper I had written on.

Ruth came to visit me, as did a crime reporter I had known for years from the *News of the World*. After many hours of interrogation from a Commander Wilson, I was remanded to Brixton.

Ruth was a personal friend of the solicitor and MP Douglas Mann, and he was engaged to defend me. On our first meeting, he told me that under the Official Secrets Act, I could expect to get 10–15 years. In the exercise yard I spoke to a couple of old friends who thought it could be even more. That night in my cell, my worst nightmares seemed to be coming true. The thought of another long sentence chilled me to the bone. How much of my life was to be spent locked in a cell? How much more could I possibly take? If I was religious, I'd say that God was taking the piss. Even with this possible sentence stretching in front of me I never grassed the guy who gave it to me. That night, there was no sleep.

The next morning Douglas Mann visited again. I knew what I wanted to ask him – can you get to the top people in the legal section of the Government? He said he could if it was important enough. I told him to try this: 'If I go to the Old Bailey under the Official Secrets Act, I will reveal in the dock the names of various prominent people in Ted Heath's Government who enjoy the favours of handsome, in some cases very young, male prostitutes. I know of a club off Park Lane where these activities take place. I also know of a stately home, owned by a Marquess, where on selected weekends the same things happen.' As a post-script to this little ultimatum I let Mann know that over the years I'd had various contacts with journalists, one of whom was Paul Foot, who knew of my character and knew to take me seriously. 'If I strike a deal of silence, and it is reneged on, copies of this information will be leaked to the press. If the powers that be put me in a cell for years, all for nicking a poxy briefcase, I will do this Government irrevocable damage.' Leaning over, I whispered to Mann: 'Let them know, if they fuck me, I will fuck them.'

The next day Mann returned. A deal had been struck. If

I pleaded guilty to possession of a stolen briefcase, the case would be heard *in camera*. I would get a lesser sentence. Would I agree to it? I nodded. This sounded a lot better than fifteen or twenty. The events that followed broke all previous precedents. Instead of being held for months on remand, as was usual, I found myself standing in the Inner London Crown court within the week. The public gallery was deserted save for two people, a man and woman. Later, I would learn that these were the civil servant from whom the briefcase had been stolen, and his wife. A sentence of two years was passed. They had kept their word. As I was taken away, Commander Wilson of the Special Branch stepped forward. 'I don't know how you swung that one, Roy, I thought you were looking at ten, at the very least.' I just smiled, Wilson's bluff didn't fool me. He had been told what was going on. As he walked away, he called over his shoulder: 'Expect a visit from me, I have some questions.' The police van took me to Wandsworth. Again. I've almost lost count of the times I've been in that nick.

At 10.30am a warder came up to me and told me I had a visitor. This was most unusual. In all my years of going to prison, I have never known anyone to get a visit in the morning hours. Another first was being taken to a prefab outbuilding instead of to the usual visiting rooms. Sitting at a table was Commander Wilson, who motioned me to sit down. He said: 'Tell me about the Russians.' Out of habit I was evasive. 'They live in Eastern Europe,' I replied. Opening a briefcase he spread some photographs on the table, which included the faces of the man and woman who had interviewed me and the contact in Hyde Park. They were all pictured innocently walking the streets of London. For a second I stared at the photos without speaking. Then Wilson pulled out a sheet of paper with an enlarged photograph of a Dorchester book of matches on it. Written on the flap was the ex-directory phone number of a Russian agent. 'This', he said, 'if shown to a jury, would have put you away for twenty years on charges of treason.' It is a stupid man who, when caught 'cold' fails to see it. I knew enough of the 'system' to know that when you are in it, a power such as British Intelligence can make sure you stay in it, no matter what the judge's sentence. Also, as a lifelong professional thief and lover of the high life, the Communist system is not one that is close to my heart. I'm closer to being a Monarchist than a Socialist. I gave him everything I could. He shook my hand when he left.

I don't know whether the information I gave him did the trick, or whether he did it by other means, but the next day he returned with an architect's plan of the Russian Consulate. Again, I helped, pointing out the two offices that I'd been taken to. This time, as he packed away his briefcase, he said: 'If anything else comes to mind, no matter what prison you are in, inform the Governor that you wish to talk to me, and it will be arranged.' Out of courtesy, but with no real expectation of getting any favours, I said that I would and thanked him. 'And, Roy,' he added, 'don't be surprised if you don't serve the full two years.' With that he walked away. I thought this was empty rhetoric. With my record, and with such a short sentence, early parole seemed an impossibility. As I was to realise later, the Special Branch Commander was a man of his word, and such covert officers wield more power than people realise.

Two days later I was transferred to Long Lartin prison in Worcestershire. Bill Perry, my old Governor from Hull was in charge, so I knew there would be little corruption and a fair regime. It was there that I first set eyes on David Wright.

Ruth continued to visit me. Due to my circumstances, our only communication had been by letter or across a prison visiting table. We had never properly talked through the subject of my bisexuality, or my love for David Barnard. She had married a man who had confessed to loving another man. In the marital problem stakes, this one was gargantuan. Once the threat of a long sentence vanished, both of our thoughts returned to our relationship. I could not deny my sexual nature. If I had been able to, I would have. To hurt Ruth was to hurt myself. I loved her as much as I could any woman, but not as much as I could a man. My love for Dave went beyond words, beyond gestures. It was inexplicable.

I told her to divorce me. She left the prison in tears. When the day ended, and all that could be heard was the footsteps of an occasional warder doing his rounds, I let my tears flow under the cover of a blanket and the night. I cried for Ruth's pain and for the illusion that had been our marriage.

You may leave your clothes at reception at the start of a sentence, but you take your testicles with you to your cell.

David Wright was a handsome young man in his mid-twenties. Although he gave me the signals that I interested him, I didn't bother to respond until the day he came to my cell and asked about jewellery. I gave him some information, and he gave me his arse. Sexually, he was a dream. I would lay back, while he worked himself up and down on my cock. He liked to do the work, and he was a beautiful young man. Emotionally there was no involvement, but once I had tasted him, I couldn't keep my hands off him.

It had long been my habit for John Wooton to hold my funds. At my expense, and on my instructions, Mary Coggles was continuing to visit Dave in Hull. At the time of my arrest, I had put the Jag in for a respray. The day I had longed for, his parole date, was fast approaching. I told Mary to collect the log book and keys and, on the day of Dave's release, to drive the Jag to Hull and present it to him, which she did. In the weeks that followed, he visited me regularly. We talked of the future – at most I'd be out within twenty months.

Dave had been in prison for twelve years. Four weeks after his release, in the spring of 1974, he was driving the Jag on the M6. He was just south of Carlisle when he lost control of the car and crashed into the motorway barriers. He was killed instantly.

Some moments are inconsequential, and some are life-changing. In the seconds it must have taken for him to lose control of the steering, for the car to hit the barriers and then to spin and flip, killing its human occupant, in those seconds, half a minute at most, my life changed irreversibly. When Dave Barnard's young body was so cruelly crushed to death, part of me also died. This was a blow from which I would never truly recover. The tragic events that were to follow, the killing of innocent people, being condemned to live out the rest of my natural life behind bars, none of that would have come to pass if that high-powered car had reached its destination. It seemed to me that I had paid a terrible price for my wrongdoings. The anger and despair that I felt from having the only real love I had ever known snatched from me, would leave me less than human. What did I care for life now? My life, any life?

17

AN IMPOSSIBLE SITUATION

As my sexual relationship with Wright continued, I started to learn more about him. As far as crime went, he was strictly petty. Sexually, he was quite promiscuous, girls as well as men. Before he turned his attentions to me, he'd been the lover of one of the Great Train robbers. There's no doubt that we just used each other. I was a thief of some standing and experience, he constantly picked my brains. His assets were his looks and his slim youthful body. It was a fair trade. His release date was well in advance of mine and, to this end, I told him of Grimshaw Hall.

There was no way that I would even consider robbing it. If Wright robbed it when I was still in prison, I had the perfect alibi. I gave him all the information he needed, how to get in, the layout of the rooms, what to take, and where it was. We agreed that he would do it and I would be paid a percentage. Before he left, I asked John Wooton to buy him a couple of suits, an overcoat and shoes. I cannot say I missed him when he left. It just meant I had to find someone else to fuck.

A couple of weeks later, I was sitting in the TV room, watching *Police Five*, when a photograph of Grimshaw Hall was shown. It had been robbed the previous night. I was pleased that Dave had pulled it off. It would get him on his feet and, if he had any scruples at all, some money should be coming my way. As time went by, no word. I had bought him clothes, set up a job for him, and nothing. Lowlife! He was just a whore.

As in all prisons there was scheming and planning for escape attempts at Long Lartin. My sentence was so short I didn't bother getting involved. I still remembered Wilson's words in Brixton 'Don't be surprised if you don't serve the full sentence.' Whether this was just the natural human state of clinging to the tiniest hope, or an inkling that he meant what he said, was difficult to tell. But I had a feeling. The feeling was borne out when, against all normal procedure, the parole board recommended me for release. Wilson, unlike Wright, was as good as his word. There's no doubt that his influence had me freed. Fourteen months after my conviction, I stepped free of Long Lartin. The parole conditions this time were for me to spend six months in the prison hostel of Winston Green, Birmingham.

The hostel room was a hovel. My prison cell had been better. I was told I would share with three other men. Empty milk bottles, discarded tins and stale food littered the room. I looked at the men I was expected to share with

– they were filthy pigs, lowlife scum. I said to the warder: 'I hope you don't think that I'm going to live in this room.' His reply was: 'You'll live where we tell you to live.' He asked me whether I needed an advance. I declined. I had £300 up my arse.

In disgust I went over the road to the nearest pub, and had some consoling brandies. Just as well barmen don't sniff the money you give them. Further along the bar were two prison officers. I watched them drinking and laughing. Who were they to dictate to me? I was a thief, yes, and when I got caught, they put me in prison. Fair enough, that was the name of the game, but forcing me to live in filth and shit with men who probably came from slums and had never got out of the habit – I wouldn't even take a piss in that place. I swallowed more brandies. They tasted nice, the pub was pleasant, it felt good to be free. Free, really, to do what I wanted. I made a phonecall. Two hours later, John Wooton turned up. He had a car and money. The screw who'd told me I'd live where he said could go and fuck himself. I got in the car and we drove up to Scotland. John dropped me off at Kilmarnock, and from there I got a train to Stranraer. Besides money, he'd brought me one of my old passports. I felt like a trip. Ireland seemed like a good idea.

From Stranraer, I could cross to Larne in Northern Ireland. My plan was to go from Larne, to Belfast, and then across the border and down to Dublin. By the time I arrived, I'd missed the last ferry. The hotel that I booked into was hosting a banquet for Scottish police. Needless to say, I stayed in my room all night. First thing in the morning, I started crossing the Irish Sea. I told Customs that I was an antiques dealer, with relatives in the country. My trip was for business and pleasure. They wished me a safe journey. After hiring a taxi to take me to Belfast, I caught the Dublin-bound train, and that night I booked myself into the Gresham Hotel. I was thinking of moving on to mainland Europe. That night, I picked up a young gay man, and took him back to my hotel room. Tired of thinking, I lost myself in his body. Once he'd gone, I slept for a long time. I felt tired. I was free, but Dave was dead. Everything I was doing, I should have been doing with him. There was no one to share the freedom with. I was free, but trapped by loneliness. I missed him terribly. His passing had torn the heart from my body – I had waited all my life for love, only to have it shown to me and then be snatched away.

My thoughts were interrupted by a knock on my bedroom door. I opened it to two detectives. I was arrested, and that day taken by police car to Belfast and back into the hands of the British authorities. I was flown to Blackpool and then taken to Walton Prison, Liverpool. As an escapee, I was put in the punishment block. My thoughts and feelings were very black. I was going round in circles and slowly disappearing. Walton is a filthy Victorian hole. I wanted to return to Long Lartin. My request was ignored and I started a hunger strike in protest. At first, they didn't take me seriously, but after four weeks living only on sips of water, my condition began to deteriorate. I got my way. I was returned to Lartin, where I served the remaining eight months of my sentence. Rather a prison cell than squalor.

I was still in that cell, when on 25 June 1975, I was given the news of my mother's death. Cancer had finally taken her. Besides dealing with my own grief, my heart went out to John. Our sense of loss was devastating. I was refused permission to attend the funeral without an escort or being handcuffed. The indignity of standing over my mother's grave in shackles was too much to bear. I sat in my cell, and prayed that she had found peace.

My release date came, and I returned to Lytham.

One day turned into another, and at times my grief overwhelmed me. There was a hole in my soul the size of an abyss. I went to stay with John. I would walk silently on the beach. With each brandy I drank, I toasted Dave. Why? Why had this happened to me? Only someone who has experienced losing the one they loved could understand the depth of my sadness and the emptiness left.

I was walking on the beach at Lytham, when I passed a seafront hotel. Wanting to make a phonecall, I walked into the reception area. They were holding a Masonic dinner of some kind. This didn't hold much interest for me, but what did catch my eye was a stack of fur coats on some seats. I spotted minks. Stepping into the phone booth, I made my call, all the time watching the receptionist at the desk. When she disappeared into the back office, I walked over to the stack of coats and, picking up a full-length mink coat, folded it and placed it inside my overcoat. I walked out of the hotel, and to my car which was parked minutes away. I was just about to drive away when I thought: 'No, an opportunity wasted, is a crime.' Going back inside, I stole two more. Doing this gave me a sparkle I hadn't felt in weeks. There is no doubt that I am addicted to stealing. It's something I show a rare talent for. I phoned Ruth in London and asked whether I could visit. She said yes. On the way south, I stopped off in the Midlands to see an old friend. I gave his wife one of the mink coats, we had some drinks, and I told him to remember that the next time I was passing he would owe me £500. He was pleased, and agreed to the sum. I carried on with my journey.

Ruth gave me a warm welcome. I gave her both the remaining minks. It was good to see her. I was lonely and seeking comfort. Next to Dave, Ruth was the only human being that I had truly been in love with. I told her that I still loved her and that I was sorry that I'd caused her so much pain. I had never meant to hurt her.

That night we made love. It was good to feel someone's arms around me, good to be held by someone I knew truly cared for me. I was inside her. Physical release eases mental torment, it releases energies and it can calm. As my body approached climax, my emotions came to the surface, the name was spoken before I knew I'd said it: 'Dave. Dave!' I called, the name of the man I loved while inside the woman who loved me. I will never forget the look on her face as she pushed me off her. It seemed that whatever my intentions, I always ended up hurting my poor innocent Ruth. You love who you love. I don't know that you have a choice in such matters.

I was sitting in John's house in Lytham when I saw an advertisement in *Country Life*, for a butler to a Lady Margaret Hudson, Kirkleton, Dumfrieshire. I sent off a letter, outlining the relevant particulars. A quiet, secluded estate in Scotland was just what I needed. I could recharge my batteries in the countryside, and think about what I would do with the rest of my life. Seven days went by before I received a reply. I was invited to travel up for an interview.

Lady Margaret was a small, ageing woman with spectacles. Kirkleton House was filled with antiques that were worth a fortune. I quickly settled into the household. I became friends with Maggie the housekeeper. All Lady Margaret's staff had been with her for twenty years or more, so I was very careful. Obviously I would rob her, but for the moment I was happy just to stay there. I enjoyed the swimming pool, the beautiful gardens, shooting with her wide range of shotguns and rifles, and I enjoyed being with Tessa. Tessa was Lady Hudson's Labrador, a beautiful dog. After a short while, she considered me her master. I fed her fresh game and gained her loyalty.

Lady Hudson often had a female companion with her, an Enid Lloyd. Mrs Lloyd did not take to me. She was suspicious. I searched her bedroom for her jewels time and time again, but I could find only trinkets, never the real valuables. In front of me, she would speak French to her friend. Knowing that I could not understand, I suspected that she made disparaging remarks about how she didn't trust me, and how she suspected me of being an imposter. I did my job well and Lady Hudson was well taken with me. What Mrs Lloyd didn't know was that when the lady of the house was drunk, which was almost nightly, I would carry her up to bed. On one occasion I laid her on her bed, and she grabbed me: 'Oh Roy, I'm so lonely, I'm so lonely.' I didn't fancy her, but I felt sympathy. I had sex with her out of the kindness of my heart. It was all I could do to keep an erection. It was an act of charity.

In my spare time, I drank in a bar nearby. I became friendly with a young man who worked there. Within weeks this supposedly straight guy would kneel at my crotch. He loved to suck my cock.

In the past, at Long Lartin, David Wright had loved to suck me. I phoned John Wooton on a weekly basis, and during one phonecall I heard Wright was trying to get in contact with me. John gave me his number. Wright had screwed me over the Grimshaw Hall job and he couldn't be trusted. He had crossed me and I am not the forgiving type. In the end, my cock got the better of me. I couldn't think of him without getting hard. I phoned the number, and invited him up.

I met him at Carlisle station and then drove him to the house. On the drive there he talked non-stop. He was in trouble with the police again in Birmingham over a robbery, but the reason he was here, seeking the sanctuary of Kirkleton House was because he'd had a rather distasteful episode with a Pakistani in a gents' lavatory. He had lured the small Asian into a cubicle with the promise of sex. What had been meant to be a mugging had gone wrong. The Pakistani ended up dead. Dave Wright ended up with me. I didn't comment on the murder of the gay Paki, his sordid little crimes were of no interest to me. I made no mention of Grimshaw Hall. All I wanted to do was have sex with him. He was low-life shite.

I told Lady Hudson that he was an old friend from way back, and had just come out of the Army after ten years of service. She invited him to do some work on the estate in return for lodgings and keep.

AN IMPOSSIBLE SITUATION

We drank her wine and spirits in our off-duty hours, and then we had sex. Most days we would swim in her ladyship's outdoor pool, afterwards we would lie naked beside it, fondling each others cocks. From the house, my ageing employer would watch us through her binoculars. I think it excited her. I could see the sun glint off the telescopic lenses. I enjoyed being watched.

I settled into life at Kirkleton. I was allowed the use of any of Lady Hudson's vehicles, including the Rolls. John was a frequent guest, coming up for shooting weekends and general relaxation. The food, wine and surroundings were of the highest quality. Each day, I inspected Lady Margaret's jewellery, which she kept in her bedroom dressing table. I knew each piece and its value. Only after I left would she be robbed. For the time being, this was as good a place as any to live. Dave continually pestered me as to why we didn't rob it straight away. I told him to be patient. If I hadn't enjoyed sex with him so much, there would have been no way I would have tolerated having him around. He made snide little comments about how he might let details of my past slip out to my employer. He ran up debts of hundreds of pounds with the local bookmaker, which I paid for him. He was an ungrateful little bastard. Yet still I let him stay.

The change in his fortunes and mine came about when I noticed a diamond ring missing from her ladyship's jewellery drawer. I searched Wright's room and found it in a rolled up sock. Later that day, we argued. In the heat of the quarrel, he threatened to expose me to Lady Hudson. Then, taking one of the cars, he vanished, presumably to the local village. If past history was anything to go by, he would get drunk, have sex with me and then apologise. Until the next time. Deep down, I despised him. Whore! I went to bed with a good book.

It was the early hours of the morning when the sound of car tyres on gravel awoke me. Wright was back. I thought: 'I'll talk to him in the morning when he's sober,' and I went back to sleep. I was woken by the explosion of a bullet entering the headboard of my bed. It had missed me by inches. In the doorway stood a drunken Wright, in his hand the smoking weapon. Drunkenly he walked towards me. He started screaming: 'We're not gonna work here anymore. We're gonna rob it tonight.' I spoke calmly and quietly: 'Of course, Dave. We will. But let's leave it till the morning.' I feared for my life. 'Dave, give me the gun, let's talk.' I tried to touch him, I wanted to get the gun. He was very volatile. Grabbing the rifle barrel, I tried to pull it from him. Dave was much younger than me, we struggled, his strength proved too much. Wrenching my hand off, he brought the rifle butt up to my face. I fell on to the floor. Laying at his feet, I pleaded with him. I told him we would do whatever he wanted. Then sinking to his knees, he started to cry. The anger became self-pity. He was sorry, he'd had too much to drink, he was upset. I took the rifle and locked it back in the gun room. Then I took Dave to his room. He was drunk and tearful. Helping him to get undressed, I climbed into bed with him. I got on top of him and fucked him, all the time thinking: 'You wanted to kill me, well I'm going to fuck you.' I didn't kiss him. That would be the last time anyone would fuck Dave Wright. I had decided to kill him. Tomorrow. I fucked him until I came, and then went back to my own room.

John Wooton arrived at the house the next day. Seeing the bruising on my face, he asked me what had happened. I told him of the situation and of my intention. First he tried to talk me out of it then, when that failed, he offered to help. John was my oldest and dearest friend. I could not let him be involved. When Dave appeared for breakfast, he was shamefaced and contrite. He apologised a couple of times. I told him: 'Forget it. John and myself are going shooting. Why not join us?' He agreed. From the gun rack, I selected the one that he'd used the previous night. Dave selected a shotgun, and took eight cartridges.

We walked up on to the moors, Tessa the Labrador joined us. John and Dave were both shooting. I bided my time. Each shot that Dave took, I counted. When his eighth cartridge was spent, I spoke. 'Is your gun empty?' He smiled and said, 'Yes.' I said: 'Are you sure? I don't want you trying to kill me again.' He thought I was jokily chiding him. He gave me a rather coy expression: 'Roy, I've explained. I was drunk and upset.' 'No Dave. You tried to kill me last night.' Nervously he took out a cigarette and lit it: 'I didn't mean anything, you know that.'

When I spoke next, the fear that I'd experienced that previous night was now reflected in his face. I said: 'I'm going to kill you.' I thought he was going to start crying again. I aimed the rifle at his head, all the suppressed anger rose to the surface, 'You robbed me of my percentage in Grimshaw Hall, you sponge money off me, I pay your debts. When I tell you not to steal anything just yet, you take a diamond ring. I'm sick of your snide little comments about how her ladyship might discover my past. You try to blackmail me, and then you get drunk and try to kill me. Well, look where your pretty little face has got you now. You've ended up on the Scottish moors, and this is where you are going to die. The only use you ever had was to be fucked.' Then I shot him in the head. For a moment he just stood there, staring. I thought: 'I've missed the bastard.' But then, slowly, a trickle of blood appeared at the left corner of his mouth. It trickled delicately down his chin. And then he fell. Walking over to him, I shot him in the chest. 'See! See, what you've made me do. You stupid, stupid, greedy bastard.' I shot him again. His eyes were still open. 'It's alright for you, your troubles are over, mine are just beginning.' He made me rage. I shot him again.

I told John to leave immediately, which he did. I dragged the body into some bushes and then went back to the house and fetched a garden spade and fork. I'd just bury him. Neither Lady Hudson nor any of the household staff were there that weekend. When I started to dig, I found that the ground was so frozen it would have taken a pneumatic drill to break it. I went back to the house to think – should I chop him up and burn him in the furnace. But then what of the smell? What if I couldn't get rid of it? Human flesh has a pungent aroma. I drank some brandies and rested for a short while. At 7.00pm I went back on to the moors and dragged his body to a small stream near to where I'd left him. When he had fallen, his arms had been outstretched and I hadn't thought to close them. Now, as I pushed them into his sides, I heard the cracking of his bones. After stripping him down to his underpants, I removed all means of identification then carefully laid him in the water.

I took heavy boulders from other parts of the stream and weighted down his body. Then I picked up whatever flower and fauna I could find and smothered his body in plants. In a daze I walked back to the house. I was exhausted, mentally as well as physically. I had never killed anyone before. Killing is very stressful, very tiring.

The next day I returned to the scene. It looked very artificial, so I went to work again. Using plants with their roots still intact, I planted more heather and ferns and whatever else I could use. A green slime was starting to form above the body, which I broke up with a stick. For the next week, I visited the watery grave every day constantly removing some things, then adding more suitable camouflage. As I worked, I talked to him. Mainly cursing him for his greed, for what he had made me do.

18
NO TURNING BACK

When Lady Hudson returned on the Monday, I told her that Wright had left to take a good job in Devon. I passed on his kind regards for the hospitality she'd shown him, and told her that he had promised to write in person, thanking her. She accepted this in good faith. On the weekend that followed, John returned. Taking a good bottle of Hock, we went back to the scene of the crime. John sat on the grass, sipping wine, and I asked him to guess where I had buried Dave. His eyes moved from bush to bush, to mounds of earth. He could see nothing unusual. I told him: 'John, he's about three feet away from you.' He put his arm round my shoulder and said: 'You've done it. You've committed the perfect murder.' A petty thief with wanderlust. No one would ask any questions. No one would ever guess.

They say that there is nothing new under the sun.

Everything has happened before. Years before, when working for the Warren-Connells, I had picked up the phone and heard the police telling my employers of my past. It wasn't the police this time. The voice had a Lancashire accent, it was a woman's, and I had heard it many times before in heavily perfumed baths. Somehow, Hazel Paterson had managed to trace me. 'He's a jewel thief. He's been to prison. He's there to rob you.' Bitch!

Half an hour later a police patrol car was escorting me off Kirkleton estate. Although she wanted me out of her house and off her property, Lady Hudson was quite magnanimous about the situation. She wrote me a cheque for three months' salary and said: 'No one will ever hear me say that you are not a fine butler.' I explained to one of the police officers that I had no transport and nowhere to stay. Using their car radio they told a hotelier in Gretna Green that they had picked up someone who had been involved in a car crash, and wondered whether they had a spare room. The police drove me to the hotel. Once there, I called Wooton. Like so many previous times, he got in his car and drove out to get me.

Since the killing, a change had taken place in my personality. There seemed to be a distance between me and the rest of the world. I felt cold and aloof towards almost everything and everyone. I had always known that I had the capacity for murder, but the act itself had caused some change to happen. I had released all that was worst in me. And once it was out, there was no way to put it back in its box. I had crossed the line. I would never be, or feel, the same again. I would say to someone who is thinking of killing: 'Don't. Whatever it is that's released, you don't want set free.'

I went to Paris for a month. I craved anonymity, I just wanted to be a face in the crowd. From France, I flew to London. I was searching for old feelings, I wanted my life to feel the way it used to. I booked into a hotel in Knightsbridge and started visiting old haunts. The places and the faces were the same, but now I was on the outside looking in. My life had numbed me.

I sought a sanctuary. I wanted somewhere to put all my things. I wanted somewhere quiet, where I could be alone with my thoughts.

Middle Farm cottage was in a small village called Newton Arlosh, a few miles outside Carlisle. I leased the cottage on a six-month holiday let, and told the locals that I was a recently divorced writer who now wanted some solitude. I don't know what I expected to find in the quiet of the cottage, but whatever it was, it never came. I had some dark thoughts – a bottle of pills and some decent brandy would end it all for me and I could escape the cold numbness that enveloped me. But suicide is not for me – my survival instinct is too strong. I decided to return to London to noises, voices, traffic, life.

Walter Scott-Elliot was that rare breed of man who, although he had enormous inherited wealth, held socialist principles. He was the Labour MP for Accrington the year that World War II ended. He then moved on to become Parliamentary Private Secretary to the Secretary of State for War. With the War at an end, they had the job of creating a peace with which we could all live. I met him in the late summer of 1977. He was eighty-two, a frail, well-spoken gentleman, and I was his new butler.

Scott-Elliot's wife, Dorothy, ran the household. Twenty years younger than her husband, she was Anglo-Indian and came from enormous wealth. She had the unpleasant habit of hitting her maids and kitchen staff. If irritated by their work, she would rap them round the legs using the walking stick that helped her mobility. Needless to say, there was a large turnover of staff. However, being a man, and being fastidious in my work and nature, as she was, we developed a friendship that went well beyond that of employer and employee. It was a shame I had to kill them.

I accompanied Mrs Scott-Elliot on all her shopping trips. Each day we would have lunch at a good hotel or restaurant. When introducing me to her friends or acquaintances, she would always say: 'Have you met my friend Roy?', never, 'Have you met my butler?'

As I settled into my new job, I started censoring all their mail. Each letter would be steamed open and inspected by me first. I knew of all their different bank accounts and all their bank account numbers. I became proficient at forging both their signatures. All phonecalls first came through me – if I didn't want them to have an awkward conversation with a stockbroker, I would give a feasible excuse. In effect, within a few short weeks, I had taken control of their lives. It was my plan to drain their worldwide bank accounts until they were empty. Then I would go abroad, to the sunshine, and retirement.

I was fifty-four years old, and overweight. Which was why, when I thought of robbing a wealthy neighbour's flat,

I needed a younger, more athletic accomplice. His job would be to climb out of my bedroom window, scale a short wall, crawl over a flat roof and gain entry. Once he was in, I would buzz the intercom and walk in through the front door..

Mary Coggles, my former 'go between' and occasional fuck, was now working as a barmaid in the Lancelot pub on the Brompton Road. She supplemented her income by indulging in part-time prostitution in the Kings Cross area. She socialised in a run-down pub called the Scottish Stores, and it was there that I resumed contact with her. I told her of my plan, and she said that a friend of hers fitted the bill perfectly. She would arrange a meeting. Two days later, I shook the hand of Michael Kitto – the worst day's work I have ever done.

Kitto was thirty-nine, smart enough in his dress and habits but a born loser. He had been dishonourably discharged from the Army and lost his wife and child. He was now little more than an itinerant. He was, however, criminally inclined and reasonably fit. He carried out the climbing I required of him, and I robbed the neighbours. Thus far I was pleased with his actions and his manner. He was quite agreeable, and sometimes I would have a few drinks with him. He slept with Mary. Sexually, he didn't interest me.

The Scott-Elliots and I were due to spend part of that summer in their house in Italy. We would leave at the weekend. Bankers, stockbrokers, and all pertinent people were informed of their arrangements. Three days before our flight date, I visited the Lancelot pub in the Brompton

Road. Mary was serving behind the bar, and I sat and chatted with Kitto. He was fascinated by my life of crime and my knowledge of jewels and antiques. He asked me whether he might take a look around the Scott-Elliots. I couldn't see a problem – the old man was on prescribed sleeping pills and would be sound asleep; Mrs Scott-Elliot wasn't due back from a private nursing home till the next afternoon. At closing time, we left for the house.

I showed Kitto what true wealth was like. Taking him from room to room, I showed him a fortune – coin collections, antiques, paintings. I suppose there was an element of 'showing off' involved, as I knew that Kitto was only a small time thief. I told him that I would steal all of it in due course. For his part, he had never worked with a thief of my stature or experience before. I could tell that he would like to be my partner, would like to impress me. Maybe that was the motivation behind the action that changed both our lives.

We were just about to enter the mistress' bedroom, when the door was opened for us. Mrs Scott-Elliot, who was supposed to be in a private clinic, was standing right in front of us. Her face displayed a mixture of shock and anger. She looked at Kitto, her voice rising: 'Roy, what is this man doing in my house at this time of the night?' Before I had chance to answer, Kitto sprang at her. Grabbing her, he smothered her mouth with his hand. His hand must also have covered her nostrils, cutting off her breath entirely. Mrs Scott-Elliot did not enjoy robust health. Having a strange man gag her with his hand, late at night in her own home, must have terrified her. To our surprise she slumped to the ground. Picking her up, we laid her on the bed. I felt for a pulse at her wrist and neck. There was none. She was dead.

I don't know what a pathologist would have discovered, and I didn't want to find out. If her death was reported, there would be a police investigation. My past would be uncovered and eventually so, too, would the missing money from their bank accounts. Even if it was decreed that my employer had innocently died of a heart attack, I would be charged with fraud and most likely the robbery of the neighbours. With my track record, I would be back in prison straight away. It would also mean the end of my little plans at the Scott-Elliots and, subsequently, no island in the sun. I needed time to think things through.

I heard Mr Scott-Elliot's footsteps in the hallway. Closing the bedroom door on Kitto and my dead mistress, I assured him that everything was OK: 'Madam awoke and wanted a drink. She has now gone back to sleep'. Only half awake, he thanked me and returned to his bed. We wrapped up my old friend in a silk bedspread. I phoned John and, in guarded language, told him what had happened. He started the drive south immediately.

When the old gent arose the next morning, I told him Madam had gone to visit friends, and she wished him to dine at his club. This pleased him very much and he didn't bother to question it.

John arrived and we discussed our options. We thought we'd have two or three days before any enquiries would be made. We would have to act quickly. We would take as much as possible, and then vanish. We summoned Mary

Coggles to the house. She was the same size as Mrs Scott-Elliot and, after putting a grey wig on her, she dressed in the Madam's clothes. I furnished her with various bank books and took her from bank to bank, where we made medium-sized withdrawals from each branch. I forged the signatures, as Coggles was barely literate, although she proved to be a more than competent actress. If Kitto had proved to be a liability, at this stage Mary was proving to be an asset. John and Kitto carried Dorothy Scott-Elliot's body, still wrapped in the bedspread, down to John's car and locked it in the boot.

It was early evening before Mr Scott-Elliot returned from dining at the Reform Club. I served him his usual whisky, which contained a crushed sleeping pill. I told him that his wife had gone to Scotland to visit friends, and he was to meet her up there. I had arranged for a car and chauffeur, and told him that I would accompany him. I then gave him another mix of sedative and alcohol, which would keep him drugged and in a state of confusion for the short time that he had left to live.

The journey north was bizarre. We drove in John Wooton's car. We sat the old man in the back seat with Mary beside him, wearing a grey wig and his wife's clothes. I told him that Mary was a friend of mine, and had been invited to join us on the trip. Kitto acted as chauffeur, and Wooton sat up front with him. I sat on the other side of my ex-master, and continued to give him shots of whisky and sleeping pills as often as I could manage. Mary talked for the entire journey. I watched the watery eyes of the old man looking at Coggles. Staring at her. He probably partially recognised the clothes and, almost certainly, his wife's wig. But in his bemused state, he was incapable of rational thought. This was just as well, because inches behind him, separated only by the moulded metal of the car boot, lay the body of his dead wife.

We stayed the night at Middle Farm, my cottage in Newton Arlosh. The next morning, before the others were awake, Wooton and I drove into Carlisle and hired a car. After transferring the dead body from his car to mine, I told him to go home to Lytham. Any more involvement could prove dangerous for him. I put a garden fork and spade into the car boot with Mrs Scott-Elliot. Kitto and I would bury her in some remote place. We drove north over the border into Scotland and stopped for lunch in the small town of Crieff in Tayside. From there we drove on to the minor desolate roads. We were about fifteen miles from Braco, when we found a likely spot. The snow-covered roads were deserted. The old man was asleep again. With Kitto taking her legs and me her arms we lifted Mrs Scott-Elliot over a dry stone wall, and dug a shallow grave in the field that lay on the other side. We covered the freshly turned soil with heather and ferns. Now that we were rid of her, the sense of relief was enormous. We drove back to Newton Arlosh, put the old man to bed, and talked.

What of him? If I was to release him and take him to relatives in Aberdeenshire, suspicions would soon be aroused – if not by him, then by others. We would need more than a few days to get at their money – forged letters from stockbrokers, forged bankers' drafts, forged letters of power of enactment would all be necessary to drain their worldwide bank accounts.

Then there were the antiques and valuables in their Sloane Street home. I had buyers, but it would take some time. I couldn't trust the old man to stay doddery and confused if I let him go. If he had a day clear of sleeping pills and whisky, he'd soon realise something was amiss. Old or not, he was still a man of some intellect. We decided to kill him. This time, we'd drive up to the Highlands. The next morning we started another journey that would end with another burial.

We stopped overnight at a hotel in Blair Athol, Tayside. We booked into the best rooms they had, and arranged for Mr Scott-Elliot to have his dinner alone in his room. The three of us drank and ate in the dining room. Mary was enjoying herself and playing the rich man's wife to the hilt. She was the coolest of all of us. In the morning we breakfasted with the man we were soon to murder. Mr Scott-Elliot paid the hotel bill by cheque. That would prove to be a mistake.

We drove north, reaching the Highland country in the early afternoon. We drove past fields, forests and streams. I was looking for somewhere that seemed ideal, when Mr Scott-Elliot awoke from one of his interminable sleeps and said that he needed to relieve himself. I helped him out of the car and watched as he walked away from the roadside to the cover of some nearby trees. I signalled Kitto to get out of the car. Together we walked up behind the urinating old man. I wrapped a scarf around his neck, and started to strangle him. He managed to get his fingers under the material, and pulled with all his might to keep his breathing free. His strength surprised me. Kitto, bloody fool that he was, just stood there and watched. The old man struggled, I lost my grip and he fell to the ground. I put my foot across his throat and barked at Kitto: 'Go and get the spade from the car boot!' When he returned, I told him to hammer Scott-Elliot's head with it. The spade crashed down on to the old man's skull, killing him. We dug a shallow grave within a copse of trees, and buried his thin, frail body. I remember saying: 'He put up more of a fight than I thought. He must have drawn strength from his noble Scottish ancestry'.

Back in the car, we started the long drive back towards Newton Arlosh. Kitto and Mary were now truly my accomplices. We had all dipped our hands in blood.

19
ACCOMPLICES AND LIABILITIES

The Highland countryside is particuarly beautiful, and we took a break at Aviemore and booked into the Red McGregor Hotel. Mary and Kitto went straight to the residents' bar and started drinking. I left them, and went to another hotel. My life, my entire life, was running and re-running in my head. I thought of my childhood, life with my mother and father in Glasgow. I had been a bright student, my teachers had expected me to succeed. I cast my mind back to Anne Philips, she, too, had thought that I had promise. I remembered Jackobosky, the young Polish captain and the first man to release my, until then, dormant, homosexuality. With his hand and head between my legs, he had stirred a drive that would help to shape my life. If I hadn't loved having sex with men, David Wright would still be alive. I truly believed that if I hadn't killed him, I would never have killed anyone. I was fifty-four years old when I shot him. All of my life I had steered clear of violence. Violence was for idiots. I was a thief, a top-class thief. For every prison sentence I'd served, there had always been a release date. If I ever appeared in front of a judge again, I would go to prison for the rest of my life. The rest of my life!

Esther Henry came into my mind, the thrill of robbing her – me and John, jewels and money filling our laps as we drove south with every police force in the country chasing us. Me, drinking with the Chief Constable of Devon and Cornwall, agreeing with him that thieves were so obvious. They had been different days. We knew that if we were nicked, we would be treated well in prison. And once we'd done our time, we'd just get out and start all over again. The Chief Constable of Edinburgh had shaken hands with me. Who would shake my hand now? I had murdered an old man. They would think me a monster. This wasn't what I had wanted. I poured the brandies down my throat, but the power of the alcohol was no match for the despair that filled me. I would only feel safe when I was out of the country, somewhere without an extradition treaty. South America perhaps?

After a while I wandered back to the hotel. Mary and Kitto were still in the bar, both quite drunk. Mary was loud and drawing attention to herself. She told me that she had been making phonecalls to her old friends in Kings Cross, boasting of the high life she was living. I told her not to make any more calls – didn't she realise what we'd done? The danger we were in? She was an accomplice to two murders, one before the act and one after. She could be looking at 10–15 years, as could John Wooton. I was in the most dangerous situation of my life, and surrounded by fools. I went to my room. Their company irritated me.

Aviemore is a beautiful, picturesque town. We decided to stay on for a few days. I took Mary up in the ski-lift and we drank in the fabulous views. As long as I was outside and busy, I could ignore the dark thoughts that were filling me. We played at being holiday-makers for a few days, before driving back to Newton Arlosh.

Leaving Mary at the cottage, Kitto and I returned to London and cleared the Scott-Elliot's home of jewellery and antiques. I visited one of my London buyers, and my former employers' property was transformed into my money. Back at the cottage, in our absence, Mary had again been on the phone, drinking and swanning around the village in her mink coat and jewels. She was now becoming an embarrassment. I told Kitto that I wasn't going to go to prison for life, on account of some cheap prostitute, no matter how long I'd known her. He agreed. We discussed whether we should kill her. I suggested that I talk to her, make her realise the gravity of the situation. She would have to change her behaviour and adopt a lower profile. Before we finished our conversation, Kitto said: 'If she's awkward, I'll just fuck her one more time and then kill her.' I left him and went to Mary.

The conversation didn't go too well. She was adamant that she was going to keep the mink: 'For God's sake Mary, the mink is evidence, it has Dorothy Scott-Elliot's initials sewn into the lining. If you return to your home in Kings Cross wearing that mink, how long do you think it will be before the police question you about where you got it? I'm going to cut up the coat and burn it. I'll buy you another one in London, one that doesn't connect you to a murder.' To my relief, she relented. I informed Kitto that he could most certainly fuck her, but he wouldn't have to kill her. Feeling slightly more at ease with the situation, we returned to Sloane Street and took more valuables from the Scott-Elliots'. My thoughts were now all focused on getting as much money together before questions started being asked about the whereabouts of the elderly socialites. Once again, we returned to the cottage.

Mary was still wearing the mink, parading around the village and attracting attention. I couldn't believe she was being so stupid, after everything I'd told her! We argued again about the coat. She had changed her mind and wanted to keep it. I told Kitto that Mary would have to go, she was going to get us all caught. He said he would have sex with her one last time and then kill her. I left him to do what he had to do.

As the evening wore on Kitto and Mary, who had both been drinking, vanished into one of the bedrooms. I sat in the sitting-room and contemplated my future. At about 3.00am Mary walked in, wearing nothing but the mink and a pair of high heels. 'Have you ever made love on a mink?' she asked. I looked at her, she was drunk. I answered: 'No. I never have.' Laying her precious coat on the floor, she lay down and waited for me. I needed some release and I have long found that physical release equates to mental release. This would calm me down and lower my blood pressure. I mounted her, and pumped away. We had sex time and time again. Until everything was gone. Until there was no more. My balls were empty and, physically, I was nearing some sort of state of relaxation. I poured myself a brandy while Mary showered.

While Mary was showering, Kitto came in. He whispered to me: 'What should we do? Should we kill her?' I didn't know why he was saying this. Earlier, he'd said he was going to fuck her and then kill her. It didn't surprise me that he hadn't. He was a weak character – weak, lazy and greedy.

Mary came out of the shower. I said: 'Mary, the coat's going. You can't have it, it's too dangerous.' She sat down and poured herself a drink: 'I'm keeping the coat. I'll be careful where I wear it, but I am keeping it, it belongs to me.' When she had gone to shower, the coat had been thrown over the arm of the settee. Picking it up, I walked to the fireplace where a roaring coal fire burned. She started screaming: 'No, no, no, no, no.' I felt my temper rise. I'd had enough of this fucking coat. Our lives were on the line! Two important people, my employers, were dead. Soon questions would be asked and an investigation could start at any time. We had robbed, fraudulently taken from their bank accounts, and my fingerprints were all over the house. I had a criminal record longer than most people's arms. And this stupid, stupid Irish bitch was prancing around in a dead woman's coat, a coat that cost thousands of pounds and had no right being on the back of this stupid cow.

'Mary!' As I shouted, I dropped the coat and picked up the poker that was leaning against the fireplace. I turned in one movement. Kitto was alert, he grabbed Mary's arms pinning them, and her, to the chair.

I smashed the poker over her head. Mrs Scott-Elliot's wig fell off and Mary fell to the ground. The blow had knocked her out. The wig had cushioned the impact preventing flesh wounds, so there was no bleeding. I got a plastic bag and put it over her head, tying it at the neck. We sipped our brandies and watched her suffocate. Ten minutes later, I checked for her pulse. She was dead. Mary, my old friend, whom I had known for almost ten years. I regretted having to kill her. Before this I'd always liked her, she had a heart of gold, did Mary.

I dressed her in men's clothes. I took a tie, without a label, and looped it around her wrist. We'd make the police think that this was some kind of lesbian murder. We put her in the boot of the car.

The following hours ticked by slowly. We waited for morning. Sleep was impossible. If you drive in the middle of the night, your chances of being stopped by the police are increased. If you don't want to be stopped, wait until the light early morning traffic has taken to the roads, then join it.

We drove over the Scottish border and searched for somewhere isolated. I considered burying her near Dave Wright's body – fitting really, two prostitutes together. I dismissed the idea because, this close to Christmas, the Forestry Commission would be out on patrol, watching for Christmas tree thieves.

We drove around and, eventually, by mid-morning we found ourselves on a deserted country lane near the village of Middlebie, in Dumfries. We took Mary's body out of the boot and tossed her over a hedge. From the hedge, we went down an embankment and put her in a small stream. There was no time for burials. She would just be another unidentified dead body – food for the fish.

John Wooton knew of the murder of Mrs Scott-Elliot, he also had an inkling of the fate of Mr Scott-Elliot. But only Kitto and I knew of the murder of Mary Coggles. There was now a strange atmosphere between the two of us.

So the three became two, our mutual friend, the woman who had introduced us, was dead. We had murdered her. Kitto wanted to be a successful criminal, I wanted out, so we went back to Sloane Street, and took everything of value and sold it. We cleared the house of all its valuables. Three carriage clocks alone were worth £75,000. I sold them for £30,000. We took all the paintings, the furs, the china, silver, everything. I knocked it all out. We were rich. All I had to do now was clear the bank accounts, stocks and shares, which would take more time, as forgeries would have to be concocted and paid for. Bogus phone calls would have to be made. Once we had these it was Heathrow, and retirement in the sun.

Sadly, that wasn't how things worked out. Two unrelated and, in the grand scheme of things, trivial incidents would turn our lives into the nightmare that they became.

Kitto and I never talked of Mary's death. If we did it was: 'Well we had to do it, she was a liability.' I was creaming in the money for the Scott-Elliot's valuables. With the owners dead, we lived in their house. It was the high life – we visited the best restaurants and went to shows in the West

End. Once the financial transactions were complete, we'd vanish into thin air.

My half-brother Don was a dirty, unkempt tramp and, we suspected, a nonce. A few years before, my ex-wife Ruth had said that she thought she had seen him 'touching' a young schoolgirl. Don was seventeen years younger than me. He had just been released from a prison in Cumbria, a three-year sentence for housebreaking. With his mother no longer alive, and him penniless, he headed straight for Lytham, and John's house.

John phoned me at the Scott-Elliots. Don worried him, he didn't really want him in the house. He asked for my advice.

Every single time I had been in trouble, which, being a lifelong professional criminal, was often, I had always been able to rely on John. He was a stalwart, a rare breed, a friend I could rely on without reservation. He was the man my mother loved. Our friendship had an almost cerebral quality. John was strictly heterosexual, I was promiscuously bisexual, yet I never loved a man the way I did him. We were soulmates, cut from the same cloth.

After Kitto and I arrived at Lytham, I told John: 'There's no way that he's going to stay here and fuck your life up for you. He'll have to go.' My first thoughts were now of murder. It was becoming the easy solution.

I brought Wooton up to date on everything that had happened. I needed John. When I had money that I wanted held, he would open an account for me, when I went incommunicado, he was my communication with the outside world. His value to me, leaving aside our friendship, was invaluable. Don would put all this at risk. John lived in a nice area where the neighbours knew nothing of his past.

I considered getting Don drunk, and just walking him into the sea, drowning him. In the end, I did drown him, but not in the Irish Sea where a washed-up body would cause police inquests. I drowned him in my holiday-let cottage at Newton Arlosh. I drowned him face down in the bath.

'John, I'll take care of it, I'll invite him up to the cottage. Kitto and I will put him to rest.' John just said: 'Be careful, Roy. Be careful.'

Dirt under his fingernails, unshaven, slovenly, I hated having my half-brother near me. He filled me with contempt. He was scum, lowlife scum. The skinny child of a miniscule Army major. We didn't even have the same father, and he had none of my mother's characteristics or nature. Lowlife, nonce, ponce, scum, I was going to kill him. I would wait for the right opportunity.

The right opportunity came on our first night at the cottage. We were all slightly drunk. Don kept asking me how much I was worth. Obviously, Kitto and I had plenty of money. Don was out to impress, he thought of me and Kitto as a team, and he wanted to join.

He said that a friend of his in prison had told him how to do a 'Tie up' using only six inches of string. He wanted to show us. I got some string from the kitchen, Don cut it into two three-inch lengths. He took his shoes and socks off, then lay down on the floor. He folded his legs up to his arse, and asked me to tie his big toes together. Then, looping his arms over his feet, he asked me to tie his thumbs together using the remaining bit of string. I did. 'See, impossible. You can't get out of it!' I looked at him, he was laying on the floor like a trussed-up chicken, with a stupid smile on his face. He thought this little trick would impress me, make me want to have him along to work with me – him, a stupid tramp!

Kitto and I looked at each other. I went into the bathroom and poured some chloroform on to a cotton-wool pad. When I went back into the sitting-room, Don was asking Kitto to untie him. Kitto was waiting for me, he knew what we were going to do.

I knelt down at his right side, Kitto at his left. I grabbed his head, and held the chloroformed pad over his mouth and nostrils. He struggled. He was fighting for his life, but Kitto held him and after some moments he lost consciousness.

I remembered that rigor mortis had proved to be a problem with Dave Wright. I filled the bath with hot water, then we undressed him down to his underwear and lifted him into the bath. He was a dirty bastard, he should have bathed more often. Just to make sure he was clean, we held him under the water for about five minutes. When we let him float to the top, he was most definitely clean, and dead. We kept him warm until it was time for him to go into the boot of the car.

20

THE BEGINNING
OF THE END

Out of the people we'd recently killed, Don was the only one with a criminal record. I knew that, if his body was found, his fingerprints would match those on police records. I didn't count Dave Wright – he was under a watery garden and would never be found. His bones would rot first.

We would have to be careful burying Don. So far only one body had been discovered – Mary's. As I had hoped, the police couldn't identify her. As far as they were concerned, she was an itinerant Scottish lesbian. A shepherd had found her on Christmas morning – hardly the stuff of Nativity plays.

We drove north for about an hour and a half, heading for the Firth of Forth. We would find somewhere completely deserted and dig a grave. The snow was falling heavily that January of 1978. This would be helpful once we had buried him, as the natural elements would cover all traces of our work. Having dead bodies in the boot of our car was no big deal. This was the third one in a matter of weeks. We stopped for drinks at Dunbar. After a few warming brandies, we carried on to North Berwick. As afternoon approached, the snowfall became heavier and driving conditions treacherous.

For obvious reasons, we couldn't afford to be in an accident or get stranded. The wise choice seemed to be to leave the burial until the next day, and book into somewhere for the night. We stopped at the Blenheim Arms Hotel.

I was later to learn the name of the manager, Norman Wright. I wished I had never set eyes on him. Wright was one of those people who is suspicious by nature. If he saw children playing in the car-park, he thought they were potential car thieves. He was fussy, and he proved to be my downfall.

A couple of weeks previously, I had told Kitto to get us some false number plates for the car. The ones we'd had ended in 999. I am superstitious and I didn't want to bring bad luck upon myself. I had told him to search for a red Granada, the same year as ours, and then to find out the name of the owner. If we were stopped by police, we would give them the right name to match the registration information supplied by the DVLC in Swansea. He was also to scratch out the old number on the tax disc and write in the new one. It wasn't a big job and he was supposed to be a criminal. Change the plates! Alter the tax disc!

But Kitto was lazy and slovenly, and he didn't have enough brains or drive to be a decent criminal. Telling me that he had done as I requested, he'd just had any old numbers done, and then fitted the reg plate to our car. He never even bothered looking at the tax disc. His stupid actions would lose us both our liberty, forever.

Norman Wright didn't like the look of us. He phoned the police to see whether they had anyone matching our descriptions on their books. Two uniformed policemen drove out to the hotel. While we ate our dinner in the hotel dining-room, they were in the car park. By the time we pushed our plates to one side, they had noticed Kitto's error. The number on the tax disc didn't match the number plates. We were just about to start on our first after-dinner brandy, when two policemen appeared at our elbows. They asked us to accompany them to the station. One of the officers drove our Granada. He was completely unaware of his passenger in the boot.

I gave my name as Roy Hall, antiques dealer from Lytham St Annes. Kitto gave his own name. The police station was almost empty, just three uniformed officers milling around. We were told we would have to wait until two detectives arrived. They were going to interview us about the car. My pockets were full of incriminating papers – phone numbers of criminal contacts, bank account numbers of the Scott-Elliots. I asked to go to the toilet and they let me go. On my own, I flushed everything down the pan. As the minutes ticked by, my fears of the car boot being opened grew. I asked again whether I could visit the toilet. Again, I was allowed to go without an escort. There was a small window in one of the cubicles. I didn't know if it would open, or if I could squeeze through it. It did, and I did. I wriggled through like an overweight eel. The thick blanket of snow that covered the ground cushioned my headlong fall. I closed the window. They'd just think I was constipated.

I ran from car to car in the police car park, searching for vehicles with ignition keys in. There were none. I walked away from the station and car park as quickly as possible. The snow was falling heavily, to my advantage. I stopped the first person I saw. I asked her whether she knew how I could get to Dunbar, my wife was in hospital there. She directed me to the home of a local taxi driver.

He believed my tale, and agreed to drive me. I settled into the back seat of his cab and hoped for the best. The drive was about ten miles. With each mile, my chances of escape grew. When he asked me which hospital, I said I'd only got the news second-hand through a phone message. He took me to Belhaven. While he waited in the carpark, I went inside, wasted a few minutes so he would think I was checking on my wife's condition, and then walked back to the car. Leaning in his car window, I asked him whether he would mind taking me to Edinburgh. To my relief he agreed. If I could get to the anonymity of a city, I was home and dry. Obviously there would have to be a change of plan – they had Kitto and my dead brother. I'd pick up some funds, and leave the country immediately.

We'd been in the car for about half an hour. Driving conditions were very slow, Edinburgh was less than twenty miles away. In front of us was the town of Haddington, and a large roundabout. It was there that I saw the roadblock, three police cars and flashing blue lights. The car door was opened, and a helmeted face peered in at me. Taking me out of the car, they radioed my description to headquarters. I fitted the picture. I felt their hands hold my arms. I sat between two policemen on the way to Mussleburgh.

At the station, detectives sat down and told me they had found the dead body of a young man in the boot of my car. I told them nothing. After some time, they gave up and put me in the cells. When they searched me, they never put their fingers up my arse. Alone in the cell, I requested a cup of water. They gave it to me. I went where the searching police hadn't. I pulled out some barbiturate capsules, my suicide kit. Spend the rest of my life in prison? I'd rather die! I washed them down my throat with the water. I remember thinking that that water would be the last drink I would ever taste.

I don't remember being moved, lifted, any of it. I have no recollection of the stomach pump. Why save the life of someone who wants to die? I had made one final bid to cheat justice, and I had failed. When I woke, my hospital bed was surrounded by doctors, nurses and policemen.

I was transferred to Edinburgh police head-quarters. All I heard was questions, mainly from a Detective Inspector Tom McLean and a Detective Chief Inspector McPherson. They quizzed me for hours. I was vaguer than a wisp of smoke. It was the pathologist from Edinburgh University, Bob Nagel, who discovered that Don hadn't drowned, but had instead been chloroformed to death. It may have been a waste of time, but I'd still enjoyed holding him down!

Each time the detectives came back to me they had more information. In another room, Kitto was talking. They knew of the cottage at Newton Arlosh. A posse of detectives and forensics moved in, and stayed for a week. By the time they left, they had lifted fingerprints from the house that matched those of the dead woman found in the stream at Middlebie and they had discovered a number of valuables from the Scott-Elliots, some with the family crest. Scotland Yard came into the picture. The Scott-Elliots had been reported missing. The pressure on us was growing and the questioning was endless.

Kitto talked. I learned that he said: 'You won't believe this, but there are two more bodies.' He made a full statement.

21
84 DAYS

I was still recovering in Edinburgh Royal Infirmary, when they next came to question me. They had all the information, they knew as much as me. Or almost! I gave them Dave Wright. Of him they knew nothing. Kitto's memory, like everything else about him, was poor; he couldn't remember the exact spots of the bodies. It was suggested to me that I should travel with the police to each location.

On the freezing, snowy afternoon of 18 January 1978 I guided the police to the shallow grave of Walter Scott-Elliot. We hadn't done a very good job of burying him. Animals had got at his body and there were bits of him everywhere. His head was still in the bushes, where we had thrown him.

Three days later, I took them to the home of Lady Hudson and the Kirkleton Estate. The severe weather had destroyed the watery garden that I had so carefully cultivated over

Wright's body. His decomposing foot was now sticking out of the water. Most of the flesh had been eaten, but the bones remained. I'd recycled him.

These field trips with the police were a welcome diversion to sitting in a cell. I was now being investigated by six police forces. They brought in a team of dogs that had been used in the Arab/Israeli war. They had been specially trained to sniff out bodies buried in sand. The ground was so frozen it took them two days to find Mrs Scott-Elliot. She, too, was badly decomposed. The only one who wouldn't have looked too bad in an open casket was Don. Ironic! In life the others had some bearing while he was little more than a tramp.

Now they had the bodies, I would await the trial and the life sentences.

Friends' houses were searched, Wooton's was searched many times. They gathered more information, and more charges. I didn't care. I knew that I would spend the rest of my life in jail, that I would never walk freely again. I wished that the bullet that David Wright had fired at me six months previously had killed me. Better death than an existence behind bars. Five months later at Edinburgh Crown Court, I was given two life sentences for the murders of David Wright and Walter Scott-Elliot. I pleaded not guilty to murdering Dorothy Scott-Elliot. The court ordered that the file on that one remain open. Kitto, who knew nothing of Wright, got two life sentences.

In October we were transferred south – a date had been set for our trial at the Old Bailey. This trial was for the murders of Mary and Don, both killed at Newton Arlosh, England. We were remanded to Wandsworth. Kitto was now growing very concerned at how many life terms he was going to get. He started talking to the police, again. In an effort to get his sentence cut, he tried to implicate John Wooton. I wanted him dead. A friend, a fellow con, offered to help me out.

If you get a dark tobacco, pour a small amount of boiling water on it, then crush it, it will secrete a brown liquid. The brown liquid is 'pure nicotine', and it is fatally poisonous. The poison was made, and slipped into his dinner. The ever-nervous Kitto suspected something and gave the food to the warders who checked it. Of course nobody knew who did it! If you're a prisoner and you grass, you should expect little else. I never touched him, but other cons poured scalding cocoa over his head.

Our trial started on 1 November. Kitto had two barristers acting for him, one of whom was the playwright and author John Mortimer. He was at the Bailey, and he had Rumpole! They tried to say that I led him by the nose, dominated him. This was rubbish – if he was frightened of me, he had plenty of opportunities to vanish. The truth was that he was weak. He was weak, and in a tight spot. First he'd tried to get his sentence reduced by giving the police Wooton, and now it was all my fault. It was his stupid killing of Dorothy Scott-Elliot that had started this whole sordid mess. If it was anyone's fault, it was his. My plan was to leave the Scott-Elliots skint but alive. I was going to take their money and run. Showing that stupid bastard around the house ruined everything. I rue the day that Michael Kitto came into my life. I hope he dies in prison, the same as me.

I couldn't see any point to a long, drawn-out trial. I

pleaded guilty to the murders of Mary and Don. When Judge Miskin QC sentenced me, he recommended that I remain in prison for the rest of my natural life: 'Only to be released if in the late stages of a terminal illness.' I smiled at him, bowed, and said: 'Thank you.'

Kitto was described as 'vile', and a recommendation was given that he serve at least fifteen years. With the trial finished, I was transferred to Hull.

There is an old saying: 'Today is the first day of the rest of your life.' It is one of those affirmations that are so popular nowadays. Whoever said that has never stood in the dock at the Bailey, and been told that their life would now consist of the banging of heavy metal doors, slop-outs, jangling of keys, food that is little better than recycled diarrhoea. Nor of the smell, that institutionalised smell that lets you know that you live in one of Her Majesty's prisons. If I was to awake each morning and say: 'Today is the first day of the rest of my life.' I would start each day crying inside. Crying for the waste. I had wasted five people's lives, and in return the Government had wasted mine.

I don't suppose there are many people who look forward to death, but I am one. My death will be my release. Not until I am dead, can I escape these walls.

As a multiple murderer, Hull proved to be a different proposition from the last time I'd been there. The screws decided to 'wind me up'. I was moved from cell to cell, each one filthy. I cannot live in squalor and filth, it makes me squirm. I would spend days cleaning them. As soon as I had got it to my satisfaction, they would move me again. In the end I'd had enough, I told them: 'Move me once more, and I'll go on hunger strike.' They called my bluff, and I called theirs.

The first thing they did was take away my radio and stop my *Daily Telegraph*. These were luxuries. If it was hunger they wanted, I would do it in silence. If they wanted a battle of wills, I would give them one. My only source of sustenance was one pint of water a day. My fast started. Jesus did forty days, IRA hunger-striker Frank Stagg did sixty. I would eventually beat them both.

The first days were the hardest. Three meals a day were brought to me, three meals a day were refused. The food would sit in front of me for one hour before they took it away. I told them I wanted to be transferred to a Scottish prison. I wanted to die in the country of my birth.

John Wooton and Ruth both continued to visit me. After fourteen days, I was taken from my cell and put into the hospital wing. My condition was now deteriorating. I started to hallucinate. The faces of the people I had killed – the Scott-Elliots, Mary Coggles still wearing that fur coat, Dave Wright, my brother Don – all their faces appeared in my cell. From their ethereal home they visited me regularly, and taunted me. I thought I was in hell. When clarity returned, I realised that I was.

I started to slip in and out of consciousness. For the most part it was the stomach pains that precipitated my return to some state of awareness. I had been in the hospital for twenty-one days when the doctors' concern grew. They told me that, if I didn't eat on the following day, I would have to be moved. They couldn't guarantee that a doctor would reach me during the night hours. At times my speech was incoherent. My body weight was falling rapidly, and I would go two or three days without passing urine.

I was taken by ambulance to Wakefield prison hospital, where they put me in the 'Special Unit.' This had housed the IRA hunger-strikers, and was separated from the rest of the ward by an iron gate and a wooden door. There was an office for the warders, a bathroom and toilet, a stripped cell, and the room where they put me. The brick walls were painted green, and there was a one-bar electric fire on the wall, which I was told, would reduce the chances of me getting pneumonia. The last occupant had been Frank Stagg.

Someone took a photograph of me lying in that bed. I must have been sleeping at the time. The next day it appeared on the front page of the *Sun* newspaper and I started to attract a lot of media interest. The Home Office declined all requests for interviews, which came from everyone, including the press, radio, TV, and even a film producer. An Oxford professor wrote to me telling me that there was always a reason to live. Gifts of food were brought to the prison gates by well-wishers. A top London barrister offered to represent me in my appeal for a move. All offers were blocked by the Governor's office, acting under Home Office instruction.

At the start of my fast, I had weighed thirteen stone, eight pounds, and now I was five stone, four pounds. An oxygen machine had been placed outside the room. I signed a form stating that, in the throes of death, I wanted no resuscitation of any kind. The authorities were off the hook. I would just slip away.

Following my arrest, the police had always been asking me some bloody stupid questions. If they found a decomposed body somewhere, they automatically thought it was me, which I found very irritating. I did the same to them – I wasted their time. I made a statement that was smuggled out to Leonard Murray, my Glasgow solicitor. In it, I stated that I had murdered two other people – an American helicopter pilot who worked off the Aberdeen oil rigs, and a car mechanic in Preston, Lancashire. Murray did some bargaining for me. A Sunday newspaper offered £25,000 for the exclusive publication rights.

I thought of Caroline, the daughter of Margaret with whom I'd lived years before. I had always stayed in touch with Caroline. She was a beautiful child. If I could do one decent thing before I died, I would try. If Murray managed to get the money from the newspaper, I instructed him to set up a trust fund for Caroline. The money would go to her when she came of age. The statement was to be made public only in the event of my death.

My blood count was the lowest they had ever recorded, and I was allowed unlimited visits. Ruth came to see me three times a week. She put vases of flowers around the room. Lord Caithness of the Home Office came too, he sat on the edge of my bed and said he was very sorry but the Home Office would not submit to blackmail. If I wished to die, then so be it. I could die here, or live here. That was my choice. I fell back into unconsciousness.

Death would have to wait. I took a bowl of soup on Christmas Day, 1979. I had gone eighty-four days without food. For all my resolve, I couldn't just let myself die. It was too drawn out, too painfully slow and the instinct to survive is buried too deep inside of me. Maybe it was the haunting hallucinatory faces of my victims. Who knows what judgement I will receive, when I finally depart this world. I dread to think my torment will continue.

As for the statement it was all lies.

22

A FULL STRETCH

Spring 1992. I am prisoner E1489, Archibald Thompson Hall. My life is shit.

It is now thirteen years since the hunger strike. I have been moved to Full Sutton, a top-security prison twelve miles north of York. I arrived here near the end of March, after spending time in Hull, and a one-night stopover in the filthy shithole that is Leeds.

For the first few weeks, there was no work. Long boring days without stimulation. My only pleasure was to walk in the exercise yard and enjoy the intermittent sunshine. Eventually, one of my job applications was accepted and I went to work under a Mrs Valerie Foster in the Education Block. My duties were light – I ensured that the staff restroom was well supplied with light snacks and tea and coffee. Foster was nicknamed 'The Witch', because of her unusual dress and mannerisms. She was a chic woman who smoked cigars, wore good perfumes, and wasn't particuarly bound by society's constraints.

For the most part the teachers were 'do-gooding' liberals whose political stance was left of centre. The more 'right wing' prison warders were not to their tastes, and this was displayed in non-aggressive but derisory ways, such as refusing to let uniformed staff eat from their catering supplies or drink from their cups. While in charge of the rest-room I put all my previous prison experience to good use. I hustled and persuaded and, within weeks, had acquired better crockery and a new coffee machine. Foster was pleased with my efforts. When she heard that I had a new job in the kitchens, she pleaded with me to reconsider. But the kitchen was better paid, and the chances for perks greater. I moved on.

As well as changing jobs, I was transferred from 'B' wing to 'F' wing. Within days, a young psychopath ran amok on the landing, stabbing a warder in the neck. Tension mounted on both sides. The warders were pissed off that one of their number had been attacked, and those cons wishing for a peaceful life wondered why a man who had already killed two prisoners was still roaming around free in an ordinary prison when he should have been in Broadmoor, or some other psychiatric unit. Because they were too lazy to do the paperwork, or someone's budget couldn't house one more man, there was a chance of a full-scale riot. The Mufti squad was on standby.

Sporadic fighting broke out between gangs of black and white cons. It was agreed that the lifers would not become involved and would let the hotheads get it out of their system. It was obvious to anyone with an inkling of insight that some of the warders wanted a riot. It would give them licence to use their sticks and settle grievances, real or imaginary.

Thankfully, the full-scale riot never came to fruition. News came through that the new lifers' wing, 'C', was ready to open. Eighty cons with life sentences were moved in – I was among them.

I settled into my new job, my new wing and my new cell. By way of celebration, I bought myself a cockatoo – Hooch. Soon this little bird became my most trusted and loved companion. That last sentence probably speaks volumes about the quality of my life.

For a few weeks all was well. The warders on 'C' wing were all volunteers. They chose to work with lifers because we are more cooperative. It gave them a chance to be constructive with their working days, to get good ideas, put them into action, and then see how all involved benefited. This is how a prison reform system should work. You can judge a society by its prison system, it is a measure of its progress along the path of civilisation.

For a few months all was well. Then, due to Government cutbacks and overcrowding, it was decided that anyone with a sentence of ten years or more would qualify for the wing. The junkies and hotheads piled in. Within weeks all the previous good work of cons and prison staff was wiped out. Items went missing from people's cells, and fights ensued. The atmosphere changed as the wing swiftly went downhill.

It's the same old story – try to save money, bung

everyone in together. One young warder with an aggressive attitude annoyed the younger prisoners so much that they set fire to the TV room, destroying it. Other social amenities were damaged. The money that the shortsighted accountants at the Home Office tried to save was spent twice over. You cannot cut corners when you are dealing with people's lives. It is a false and stupid economic strategy.

Such is life in Full Sutton. Will I end my days here? I hope not.

17 July 1992. Today is my sixty-eighth birthday. This day, my birthday, will be like every other day.

My cell door is unlocked at 6.30am. The officer is also a man of moods. In an effort to make the most of my lot, I say pleasantly: 'Nice summer morning, isn't it?' His replies are often less than courteous, the most common being: 'If I want a fucking weather report, I'll phone the BBC.' Nice man.

I report to the kitchen for work. For a man of my age, the hours are long and I will not finish until 5.30pm. Tiring though it might be, eleven hours working is better than eleven hours sitting in a cell.

My tasks are menial. I wash up, clean working surfaces, peel vegetables. I don't mind doing these simple chores. In action, I can cultivate a mental detachment. If I'm scrubbing a pan, I'm not thinking of the past or the future, for those moments there is only the pan. The killing of time is an art form. It is something I have developed. This simple philosophy was taught me years ago by an old con.

He told me that if I could discipline my mind in this way, there was a good chance of leaving prison with my sanity intact. Although I will never leave, I am grateful to that man. It is now habit. I get through the day by applying this 'no mindedness' to all that I do.

From 6.00–8.00pm we can, if we choose, watch TV, have a game of snooker, play table tennis, or just socialise. If the weather is nice, I walk in the yard, if inclement I will chat with friends or listen to BBC Radio Four. We have access to a kitchen. It is my chance to eat. The diarrhoea that the authorities dish up is incapable of keeping you healthy. Also, it tastes like shit. Most evenings I will cook a chicken, or a couple of nice chops. We take the food to our cells. Together with a couple of friends I will sit down to a nice meal and a few glasses of hooch – homemade wine. This is the nearest we are allowed to get to civilised behaviour. Just because I have killed does not mean that I am a mindless monster. I am capable of intelligent discussion. Although I don't like to voice it, I am also capable of remorse. That I will save for the afterlife. For now, I need to survive. It is not good to show weakness in a place like this.

The TV room is nicknamed the 'Beggar's Arms', and is always full of drunken young idiots. I rarely watch TV. I want to go to the Lifers' Unit at Kingston, outside Portsmouth. I am a 'natural lifer', one of only two in the prison. If I was free I'd be on a State pension, so why should I have to serve my time with fools who are only doing ten years? They have a release date, they get drunk, shove that filthy white powder up their noses and behave like animals. Men who will never be free have a different attitude. For us a peaceful, hassle-free, existence is the best that we can hope for. You have to make the most out of what you've got. A nice meal with a couple of friends, some glasses of hooch, that is what gives my life some quality. Nowadays, I think about almost everything. I have little else to do. I try to make some sense of my life.

Years ago in prison, cons would do all they could to make their life a little more bearable. This was in the days when the regimes were brutal, and drugs unheard of. Today's cons don't seem to exercise any sense of discretion. Instead of drinking homemade booze quietly in their cells, they wander out drunk on to the landings. This, in turn, instigates more cell searches. Those of us who have carefully hidden hooch have it poured away, and are put on charges. Why make life harder than it need be? These young idiots have no common sense or consideration. Fights and knifings are commonplace.

8.00pm is 'lockdown'. I am grateful for the fatigue that I feel. My weary body will now accept sleep easily and in sleep there is escape. The dream state is not subject to material laws, in my dreams I am always free.

July 1994. After months of pestering and filling in forms, the Governor of the Lifers' Unit at HMP Kingston has granted me a month's probationary stay. This will be a quieter prison, a more relaxed regime. It has been built especially for people like me, for those getting on in years, for those whose fate it is to die within the prison system. If it is possible to get excited about moving to a place of incarceration, then I am. I will not write again until my return.

August 1994. I returned to Full Sutton yesterday morning. To say that it filled me with a sense of dread and despair would be an understatement. I have been sitting and thinking for hours. Radios have been blaring all night. Sleep was impossible. Young cons have been arguing, the screams of their abusive threats reaching everyone's ears. I have friends on the outside petitioning for my move and Lord Mackintosh has promised to speak up on my behalf. He is a true gentleman. There has been a change in my thought patterns – instead of blotting out the present by thinking of the days when I was a free man, I now dream of the Lifers' Unit at Kingston. It is amazing how a human being's expectations of what constitutes happiness can change. As a young man, happiness was the adrenalin surge of a theft and the high life that immediately followed. Now it is to watch TV in the privacy of my own prison cell, and to be free from the air of violence. If I had felt this way years ago, if I hadn't been so consumed by greed, the tragic killings that ruined so many lives, including my own, would never have happened. Perhaps I have learned. Perhaps I have changed.

Kingston was all that I thought it would be. There was a sense of peace there that isn't prevalent in short-term prisons. There is cooperation and even a sense of camaraderie between prisoners and warders. It is the penal system's equivalent to a hospice. The thing that struck me most was the absence of violence and drugs. There you are allowed, at your own expense, to have a TV in your cell. You can walk peacefully in the grounds. I pray and hope that my transfer will be granted.

The warning that they gave me on my arrival – any trouble and I would be straight back to Full Sutton – was not necessary. This is all that I want.

23
THE SPIRIT
IS WILLING

Another birthday – 17 July, 1995. Another long year has passed. I work in the kitchen, wander around aimlessly, have a meal, then 8.00pm lockdown. On this oh-so-special day, I have some birthday drinks with Gary Griffin and Rab Harper. Happy birthday!

18 July, 1995. I wake up feeling a bit pissed off. The cell seems small. I feel a rage coming. Ever since the day that I murdered Wright, I know when anger stirs inside me. I hope I'm left alone.

Tinny radios have been blaring out music for half the night. The walls hem me in more than the constant noise around me. I am a prisoner of my own sounds, my own sweat. How much sitting in a cell can a man fucking take!

There is a bad feeling in the kitchen. A Rasta, doing eight years, has an argument with a friend of mine.

19 July, 1995. The atmosphere in the kitchen is tense. I will do my job and mind my own business. Prison politics is something I have learned to avoid. During the 6.00–8.00pm social period, the bad feeling of earlier finally moves from words to action. My friend is beaten up by the Rasta. Let's hope that's an end to the whole affair. All the workers in the kitchen have been affected by this. We all knew how it would probably end. At 71 I want no part.

20 July, 1995. I am stopped on the landing by an old friend of mine. He is acting as mediator. He wants to know whether I am thinking of taking any revenge over the beating of my friend. I tell him I am here for the rest of my life, all I want is peace and quiet. I have no wish to become involved.

21 July, 1995. The stupid bastard Rasta wants to stab me! Why? I said I didn't want any trouble! I have heard whispers in the kitchen. He is telling people he's going to 'stick' me anyway. He's paranoid. The threats make me angry, doesn't the stupid young bastard realise that I have nothing to lose? I'd slit his throat just as soon as look at him. It makes no odds to me.

The whispers continue. I hear he has a blade. I take a knife from the kitchen, the biggest one there. If he fucks with me, it will be to his lasting, possibly dying, regret.

That evening I see him in the social room. As soon as he walks through the door our eyes lock. My knife is hidden in a folded newspaper. For the moment I don't show it. He stands there watching me, his hands in his pockets. I am the first to speak, I motion towards his pockets with my eyes: 'Have you got something in there for me?' The confrontation has started. Now I am ready. This young black guy, a man forty years my junior, the one insistent on causing trouble, doesn't answer. I have been in and out of prison for fifty years. I know that if you are shown to be weak you are finished. I slide the knife out from under the newspaper. Standing up, I walk over to him. I lift up my T-shirt and show him my fat seventy-one-year-old belly: 'Go on, stick whatever you've got into that. Go on!'

I show him my knife: 'But be sure of one thing, you won't leave this room alive.' I look him straight in the eyes and smile. The smile is a death smile, colder than ice.

His hands come out of his pockets without a knife. 'No. No trouble, man. I just wanna keep me head down and do me time.' I thought he was going to apologise for breathing. The old, like the young, can be vulnerable in prisons. Now that I have the upper hand, I give my coup de grâce. With my left hand I unzip my fly and pull out my cock. The fool who had started all the trouble looked at it for a second, then, unsure of what to do, stared at the wall opposite. I flop my flaccid penis around in my hand, my eyes still boring into him: 'Is this what you want? Do you want to suck my cock?'

With his head bowed he walked away. My tactics had been severe, some would say over the top. But neither this man nor any man watching would give me trouble without good cause. The old one survives.

August, 1995. I am told that my services in the kitchen are no longer required. My job is being given to a younger man. They have retired me.

Perhaps their plan is to bore me to death. Without a job, I am left only with my memories, my cockatoo, and my friends.

My sexual needs are not as prodigious as they once were, but occasionally opportunities arise. Due to my experience and open-mindedness, I am viewed differently from the run-of-the-mill rabble. Young men, when they have been locked away for a long time sometimes seek a father figure, a human being, without the crass macho façade portrayed by so many in here. Sexuality is a fragile thing. Many people harbour fantasies they are frightened to voice. If they awarded Olympic medals for sexual repression, the British would win gold.

A short while ago I noticed a young man in his mid-thirties. We were both having visits, me from an old friend, him from his wife and children. When it was time for visitors to leave, I watched this young con kiss his gorgeous model-like wife passionately. He hugged and kissed his two young daughters. To all intents and purposes this was a heterosexual family man doing time.

A short while later this same man knocked on my cell door and asked whether he could have a word with me. I felt the conversation was slightly false, as if he wanted to say something but couldn't summon up the courage. Eventually the small talk finished and he asked me whether there was anything he could do for me for £5. Now, I knew that he knew of my ambiguous sexual orientation. They all did. I said to him: 'What do you mean anything?' He looked into my eyes and repeated: 'Anything!' Now, we both knew what we were discussing. This young man was finally coming to terms with the fact that, under certain circumstances, he was willing to have gay sex. He wanted to.

I told him that if he wanted to do it, he should do it. But not for £5, why prostitute himself? It turned out that the money was just an excuse, an acceptable way of saying something that his conscious mind had difficulty accepting. His real fear was that the other cons would get to hear of it. I assured him that I was the soul of discretion. He nodded, a nod of compliance. I keep a wooden wedge in my cell for reasons of privacy during the hours that the doors are unlocked. I told him to put the wedge in the door. An hour after this family man had kissed his wife goodbye, he was having sex with me. I say again, sexuality is a fragile thing, shaped by we know not what. It is wrong for any of us to judge consenting adults. Under slightly different circumstances it could be us.

When I walk out of a visiting-room I never look back. In my mind, I compartmentalise my contact with the outside world. My visitors, my friends out there, have no way of understanding my life in here. I enjoy their company, I like to hear how things have changed, it's like hearing second-hand about heaven.

Full Sutton has its fair share of 'faces', people of known repute. Ronnie O'Sullivan Senior, father of the famous snooker player, is on the wing. He's a London villain of some stature. Porn, robbery, murder, he was, as they say, 'at it' in quite a significant way. He is a pleasant man with no interest in prison politics. I like him.

Jeremy Bamber arrived from Long Lartin. This is a man who is a problem for the authorities. He was found guilty of murdering his parents, his sister and her two children in order to inherit half a million pounds. He is notorious, hated by most cons. He has been subjected to various attacks and beatings. In order to survive he has got himself super fit and, in a one-on-one situation, he is a dangerous man. He claims he is innocent. That is not unusual, many do. Personally I keep an open mind, I have seen many men win appeals. When asked about him, I state my opinion – leave him be. Which one of us can be certain of knowing the truth?

Three of my closest friends here are Hugh Docherty, Eddie Butler and Joe O'Connell, all members of the Provisional IRA. In 1975, while on the run from the police, they entered a flat in the Marylebone area of central London, and took hostage the two occupants. It became known as the Balcombe Street Siege. They were each sentenced to thirty years. These men are not really criminal types – when they were active in the IRA they were young men filled with the fire of political activism.

Britain imposed its will on Ireland and the Irish. They put Protestants in a Catholic country and annexed it. What do they expect? With any country it would be a stupid thing to do, but, knowing the Irish temperament, the Gaelic fire, it was a stupendously idiotic thing to do. As long as the British are in Ireland the Troubles will continue. The sentences they dish out to the young Irishmen who take up arms against them are ridiculously harsh. They say that for offences committed on the mainland they must be imprisoned on the mainland. But, if as Westminster claims, part of Ireland is British soil, then why not at least let them serve their sentences back in Ireland, where it would be easier for their families to visit them? Thirty years! Thirty years is an incredibly long time. A just legal system should be a compassionate legal system. Young hotheads turn into mellow middle-aged men. They have been behind bars for twenty years, it is time for mercy. Time for clemency. Let the sons of Ireland return home. They have paid the price for their indiscretions. Lack of mercy just fuels hate in those to whom hate comes easily. By its very actions the British Government ensures that the Troubles will continue.

If friends are important on the outside, they are even more important on the inside. In Gary Griffin and Tony Murray I have two of the best the world could offer. Gary is a young man serving a life sentence for murder. The judge gave a recommendation of fifteen years. That would have been a fair sentence if he had actually murdered anyone, but he didn't. His crime, and I use the term in its loosest possible sense, was one of misguided loyalty. Gary's employer was a jealous man whose wife had taken up with an Arab. One evening his boss, with Gary in tow, went to visit his estranged wife. Unbeknown to Griffin, his boss was carrying a knife and had murderous intent. The wife was stabbed to death. Gary's mistake was that, once the deed was done, he failed to phone the police and distance himself from the crime. Along with his employer he was found guilty and given life. In prison Griffin uses his time constructively. He is studying for an Open University degree and keeps clear of drugs and trouble. He is principled and moral. The police and the court's assumption that he is a murderer is just that – an assumption. And it is a mistaken one.

Tony Murray is a completely different kettle of fish. A self-made millionaire from Liverpool, Tony owns pubs and nightclubs. His twelve-year sentence is at the moment under appeal, so I won't say too much about it. Suffice to say, he is accused of being a drugs baron. Tony is a kind man. He is a working-class kid from the inner city who ended up as a neighbour of Manchester United boss Alex Ferguson in the leafy suburbs of Cheshire. If Tony Murray is guilty of the charges levelled against him, one thing is certain, he would never condone drugs being sold to children. He would never encourage people to take drugs for the first time.

Drugs are now part of the fabric of modern society – where there is a demand, a supply will sooner or later show itself. For a man who is basically just an entrepreneur to be given a longer sentence than many rapists and paedophiles is disgusting.

January, 1996. Age is a terrible thing, everything starts to go south and everything starts to fail. Now, it is my eyes. After seeing the prison doctor on a number of occasions an appointment is made for me to go to York Infirmary and have a preliminary examination. They tell me I have a cataract in my right eye. A date for the operation is set. I am pleased something is to be done, as blindness frightens me. To be blind at any time is bad enough, but to be without sight in a place like this would be hell. Half of my vision is very blurred.

The morning of the operation has eventually arrived. The warders who are to act as my escort come to my cell. I am given a light-blue cotton suit to wear. The material is no thicker than that of summer pyjamas. I am taken out of the prison under heavy escort. They must think a 72-year-old half-blind man could overpower them and outrun them. The situation is made even more ludicrous and more humiliating by the fact that the trousers they have given me are so ill-fitting that they keep slipping down. With my hands handcuffed and connected by a chain to a warder in front of me, I cannot even pull them up myself. Every few feet, one of the warders behind me has to pull them up. The half dozen young men who surround me are all wrapped up well against the bitter weather. The wind cuts right through my thin cotton suit and I shiver uncontrollably.

This is the first time I have been outside a prison in years. I am a pensioner in poor health who will never be freed. The chances are I will never see the outside world again. But would they allow me the dignity of wearing clothes that fitted me, or take the chains off? No. I walked into the hospital with my trousers falling down every few paces, handcuffs on show, and chained to a guard. I was like a sideshow freak, attracting stares from all I passed. I don't ask for sympathy, I don't ask to be released, just for a little kindness, just to be let to walk down a hospital corridor without being treated like a wild animal. I'm surprised they didn't put a face mask on me like Hannibal Lecter. Even on the operating table, the chains stayed on.

THE WICKED MR HALL

If the prison authorities shamed themselves by their behaviour, the civilian doctors and nurses didn't. Doctor Jacobs and his staff were most courteous and kind.

Back at the prison I go straight to my bed. Friends call on me to see that I'm alright. The prison doctor never came near me. As my eye heals, it weeps continuously. I can't even get any cotton wool with which to dab it. In the end, an old-time warder kindly brings me some from his own home. I am very thankful for this small act of kindness. The years of incarceration have instilled in me a humility that I never had as a young man. I am aware of the change.

EPILOGUE

From my cell window, I can see the prison sports fields. Some weeks have passed and spring is in the air. Today I walked in the sunshine for an hour. It was very pleasant. Inside the wing things haven't been so good. I have been fined twice and put on charges for having homemade hooch. I watched them pour it away. After making it, I'd moved it from one place to another. Drinking it lets me lose myself in thoughts for a few hours. This place is riddled with drugs – heroin, cannabis, cocaine – yet an old man's homemade wine is poured away. Do the authorities really think a 72-year-old, quietly drinking wine in his cell, is a threat to them?

My friend Hughie Docherty is also getting grief. His cell has been searched on a number of occasions. Hughie is one of that rare breed that can survive without drink or drugs. The screws have even smashed his toilet bowl. They are annoyed at not being able to find anything. The reason? Hughie is IRA. Even though he's been in prison for twenty years certain warders blame him personally for the Canary Wharf bombing. He has been put in the punishment block for refusing to squat and let them search his anus. A man who has done nothing wrong refuses to let an angry prison warder stick rubber-gloved fingers up his arse and he is punished for it.

In this place it is hard not to feel anger. I have just heard that my proposed transfer to Kingston has been turned down. They have waited two years to tell me that I will end my days here. The dream of having my own TV set has died. Murdering paedophiles such as Myra Hindley and Ian Brady have them. Yet I have been refused. This is my life.

April 1999. I have not written anything for three years. The time has passed slowly.

I wait for death; but when will I die? It is ironic that I have a strong constitution, I could live to be 100. Now at the end of my life I am paying for my sins – I am too old to work, I spend all of my life alone in my cell. Soon the century will change, I am a man out of my time, all of my old friends are dead, no one visits me. I am rotting towards the millenium.

In the summer of 1997, 'E' Wing went up like a powder keg. The atmosphere was bad. The screws were pushing their luck. Full Sutton is a top-security prison, and if you take liberties with the people who are housed in such places, you must expect a reaction.

EPILOGUE

To be honest, I found it exciting. There were fires, and they took over the prison. The people who were my oppressors lost their power, and they no longer had control. It made an old man happy.

I stayed in my cell throughout the whole thing, which lasted for three days. We were told that the television cameras were outside. For those three days, we were an independent state. We might as well have had our own government, and within the confines of the prison walls we were free.

When the anger subsided, the authorities surveyed the carnage, before coming to the obvious conclusion that 'E' Wing was uninhabitable. We were all moved into the system. I was transferred to the south coast and back to HMP Kingston. For something that I had previously perceived as a dream move, the reality proved very different. I no longer had the finance to purchase my own television, and I made no friends. I experienced loneliness on a new level. I constantly asked for a transfer and after a few months they moved me to HMP Garth in Lancashire. This proved no better, and I wanted to go back to Full Sutton where I at least had some old friends. It took a further eight months for me to come full circle, and in November 1998 I returned to the prison I now regarded as home and the place where I will die.

No one visits me. My few close friends still look out for me in my old age, but I have no part to play in the twenty-first century. Only death can release me now, and I will wait for it as patiently as I can.

To any criminal, to anyone who thinks they might have

the capacity for murder, to anyone similar to myself, I would urge you not to do it. Think again. In the final analysis my life is an impoverished nightmare.

Let me be a lesson to you.